Collecting
Royal Winton
CHINTZ

Muriel M. Miller

Francis Joseph

ISBN 1-870703-12-X

© Francis Joseph Publications 1996

First impression

Published in the UK by
Francis Joseph Publications
15 St Swithuns Road, London SE13 6RW

Typeset, printed and bound in Great Britain by
E J Folkard Print Services
199 Station Road, Crayford, Kent DA1 3QF

ISBN 1-870703-12-X

Acknowledgements

Very few books can be written without the aid of other people, and I would like to thank the following for all the help they have given me.

The first on the list has to be my husband, Dave Barker, without whose support during the long, and sometimes tedious years of research, the project would have foundered.

I am greatly indebted to Stella Colter, Leonard Grimwade's granddaughter and daughter of Charles Donovan Grimwade for the loan of personal papers and memorabilia. I also owe thanks to Mr A G (Geoffrey) Grimwade for his research into the family tree and to his wife, Ruth, for her hospitality.

Lily Bell, Florence Dennis, Dolly Draycott, Albert and Sybil Stevenson, all worked at Royal Winton during the 1930s and gave me added colour for the Grimwades' story, while Mrs Beth Davis, whose husband was on the Board of Directors, offered invaluable assistance with early catalogues. Mr Philip Plant, son and grandson of James Plant and James Plant Senior, was also more than helpful. All the above have been generous with their time, and made me welcome in their homes.

Many people have lent me pieces of chintz ware from their own collections and I would like to thank Joy Humphreys of the Angel Arcade in Camden Passage, London, Beverley of Church Street, London, Diana and Ken Glibbery of the Royal Winton International Collectors' Club, and Sheila and Roy Selby.

I am also grateful to Fritz Mueller of Vancouver in Canada for sharing with me valuable information on Royal Winton shapes.

View of the Finishing Warehouse taken in 1906

Contents

Yours faithfully
Leonard L Grimwade

Chairman of the Board.

Introduction

About twenty years ago, I bought a cottage-shaped teapot. The name stamped on the bottom was that of Royal Winton. Soon afterwards I began collecting pretty chintz plates and again, the backstamp was Royal Winton.

As my collection grew, I became intrigued. Who was Royal Winton? Where was the factory based? How old were my plates? And where could I find the answers to my questions?

A few years later I entered the world of antiques. As I learned more about ceramics, I bought reference books. These helped me to date the chintz ware I'd bought and informed me that the factory using the Royal Winton backstamp was known as Grimwades and was based in Stoke-on-Trent in Staffordshire, but I found out little more than that. Books were available on other pottery manufacturers, but none on Grimwades.

Finally, in desperation, I decided to write the book myself. I was a freelance writer and used to researching facts. And so began the odyssey that was to take me six years. It was a slow process, frequently interrupted by other writing projects. I was also hampered by the fact that, after the take-over of the Winton Potteries by Howard Potteries in 1964, all catalogues and pattern books appeared to have been destroyed. Indeed, one Royal Winton worker who had been employed at the time told me that the main pattern book had gone 'walk-about' during the move, and that all catalogues had been burned.

The museum at Stoke-on-Trent, although helpful, could find no documentary information and neither could the present day Royal Winton Company.

I was lucky enough to be put in touch with Stella Colter, the granddaughter of Leonard Grimwade who was the founder, chairman and managing director of the firm until his death in 1931, and she opened a great many doors to me. Also at this time I managed to locate the whereabouts of several Grimwades catalogues which were to be of immense research value. The latest of these catalogues is dated 1930, when the Royal Winton chintz ware was in its infancy and no other documentary evidence, apart from short reports in *The Pottery Gazette*, have been uncovered.

This means that there are several gaps in information about chintz. There are shapes I have been unable to identify, and shape names found in catalogues which I have been unable to match to manufactured items. Also there are patterns mentioned in *The Pottery Gazette* which do not appear to exist, neither here in the UK nor in America, Canada or Australia.

Some patterns have been found which have no identifying names; these have been given names set within quotes, such as 'Violets', for ease of reference. There are also patterns which appear only outside the UK.

I have to apologise for and correct previously published errors. In an article written by me which appeared in *Antique Collecting* in June 1992, **Bramah** was listed as a Royal Winton pattern. In fact, Bramah was made by W R Midwinter Ltd. In addition, the **Clevedon** pattern was wrongly printed as *Cleveland*. Also now in doubt, and open to further investigation, is the *Japan* pattern which cannot definitely be ascribed to Grimwades.

In addition, it has been established that the pattern christened 'Blue Anemone' is, in fact, **Chintz**, and the pattern called *Rose Violet* is **Rose du Barry**.

Perhaps the publication of this book will bring further facts to light regarding Royal Winton chintz ware and I would be happy to hear from readers having fresh information. In the meantime, happy collecting!

Muriel M. Miller

The Company

The firm of Grimwade Brothers was founded in 1885 at the Winton Pottery, Stoke-on-Trent, by Leonard Lumsden Grimwade and his elder brother, Sidney Richard. The factory originally consisted of a shed sited between two rows of cottages but business was brisk and it was not long before the firm expanded.

In 1887, the Winton Hotel was built featuring new showrooms. It was sited close by Stoke Station and was convenient for visiting buyers who travelled by rail. The company's turnover doubled each year and by 1890, a flourishing export department was established with the company taking a London showroom at Ely Place, Holborn.

To cope with this development of trade, a new Winton Pottery was built in 1892. This was a large building set on the main road and had the added advantage of being only a three minute walk from Stoke Station. The building had a frontage of 180 feet and a four storey elevation. It contained some of the most up to date equipment to be found in the potteries at that time and, over subsequent years, the area at the rear was built up with a network of kilns, ovens and workshops. The total area covered was almost two acres.

The showrooms were sited in London at 3-5 Charterhouse Street, Holborn Circus and by 1889, had moved to Ely Place, Holborn.

In March 1900, the Stoke Pottery, owned by James Plant, was acquired with Plant being given a place on the Grimwades Board as a director. The Stoke factory was adjacent to the Trent and Mersey Canal and, apart from the large range of ovens and kilns, also included complete equipment for milling the raw materials, including flint and Cornish stone. The three potteries (Grimwade Bros, Winton Pottery and Stoke Pottery) were then amalgamated under the title of Grimwades Limited with Leonard Grimwade as chairman.

In that same year, the Grimwade brothers left Ely Place and purchased the lease on 13 St Andrew Street, a corner site at the conjunction of St Andrew Street and Shoe Lane in Holborn Circus, London. Winton House, as it was known, then became their main showroom.

Back in Stoke, Leonard Grimwade experimented with new methods of kiln-firing and developed enamel firing of high quality with the use of Climax Rotary Kilns.

New showrooms were erected at the Winton Pottery in Hanley in 1906. To achieve these, three cottages in Newland Street were pulled down and a three-storey building was erected. It was opened by the Mayor of Hanley on the 25th of October.

Expansion continued at a great pace. Brownfield's Works, carried on by The Upper Hanley Pottery in Woodall Street, Cobridge, were acquired in 1906, the factory being 'particularly adapted for trade with

Canada, the United States of America and other important foreign markets'. Later in the same year, Atlas China (formerly David Chapman & Sons) in Wolfe Street was purchased, enabling the company 'to cater for their many customers who required high-class China Tea Sets at moderate prices especially suited to a cultured taste'. The Heron Cross Pottery at Fenton, owned by Messrs Hines Bros, was an extensive earthenware pottery with extra large ovens and several enamel kilns and this was bought the following year, adding considerably to the company's facilities. (It was later sold to Cartwright & Edwards in 1916.) Grimwades also acquired the Rubian Art Pottery Ltd in 1913.

Export trade was also on the up with the company having agents in Australia, New Zealand, Canada, India, South Africa, South America, United States of America, Sweden, Norway and Germany. By 1920, Egypt had been added to the list.

In 1908, Leonard Grimwade bought shares in the Chromo Transfer and Potters' Supply Co Ltd. This company, which was situated at one end of the Winton Pottery factory, provided 'chromo and lithographic transfers, ceramic colours, potters' materials, glazes and the like'. They were also responsible for the development of 'Duplex' paper, a thin printing tissue which made the lithograph process easier.

Leonard Grimwade also purchased the patent rights of the Grimwade Rotary Display stands around 1913. These were 'Made of finest steel, double-plated metal parts, stained wood shelves' and could accommodate '12 half tea sets, 12 cover dishes and plates, or 12 ewers and basins'. The stands were used for shop display and economised on space. Also, 'ware can be displayed so effectively that assistants are able to increase sales and serve customers far more expeditiously.'

Patent 'Ideal' Display Blocks & Wires were also acquired by Grimwades, and these were used to show tea cups and saucers to advantage, or sets of jugs, blancmange moulds, teapots and butter dishes. Smaller blocks were used for trios (cup, saucer and tea plate) or samples of dinner ware. Wall mounted hardwood strips were available for displaying wash stand sets.

In 1920, a laboratory was set up at the Victory Works at the Stoke Pottery. This was run under the supervision of Leonard Grimwade's son, Charles Donovan, who had for some years been in charge of a large tile and brick works at Tongshan, North China. Grimwades anticipated cheaper production improved quality and they tested new methods and new materials 'so that we may be in a strong position for future business'. Also that year, gas fired tunnel ovens were pioneered by Grimwades. These had been laid just after the Armistice and were opened in September 1920. The huge tunnels (298 feet in length) were capable of turning out as much ware as six full-sized ovens.

The railway strike in 1920 affected delivery of goods to customers, so Leonard Grimwade purchased a new 'Karrier' motor lorry for a cost of £1300. This proved so successful – 'No breakage – no delay – no incivility on the part of carters and a lessening of serious inconveniences' – that the company aimed to build up a complete system of motor transport during 1921.

In 1929, a new showroom was set up at Winton House in Stoke-on-Trent. It was named the Victoria Showroom and was to be used for tableware of all kinds, especially bowls, vases and jardinieres. 'It will be used exclusively for representative selections of the latest and most artistic productions', ran the advertisement. It was to be the third showroom at Winton House. The Royal Showroom catered for the dinner ware, toilet ware, teapots and coffee sets and so on, while the Excelsior Showroom was devoted to clearance lines suitable for sales.

Leonard Grimwade died in 1931 with James Plant (Senior) dying in the same year. Plant's son, another James, took over as Managing director in 1933 and he died in 1962.

In January 1964, the company was taken over by the Howard Pottery Co Ltd of Shelton. Part of Grimwades production (50% of which was exported mainly to Australia, Canada and New Zealand) was moved from Stoke to Norfolk Street, Shelton, with the remainder being transferred some weeks later. The name Royal Winton was kept.

The ware was highly ornamental and much of it was hand painted. There was also a great proportion of gold fancies made, with a specially air conditioned room being set aside for the application of the gold. Orders went out all over the world. Canada formed the largest overseas market, with Australia and New Zealand close behind. A new 'Royal Winton' tie-on label had been designed and this was printed in the Howard colours of chocolate brown, white and grey.

Between 1964 and the present day there have been several successive owners of Royal Winton. Pentagon Holdings acquired Howard Pottery in late 1960, and supplied Taunton Vale Industries with ware. Pentagon itself went on the market in 1973 and was bought by its erstwhile customer, Taunton Vale Industries Ltd. In 1979 the Staffordshire Potteries purchased Taunton Vale Industries and in 1986 were themselves taken over by Coloroll (Ceramics Division). Despite all the various takeovers, the name Royal Winton was kept alive. When Coloroll was declared bankrupt in 1990/91, there was a management buy-out for Royal Winton. In 1993, the company was purchased by Spencer Hammer Associates and a new company formed: Burnan International Limited. They are still trading as Royal Winton.

Leonard L. Grimwade

Leonard Lumsden Grimwade was a man of extraordinary vitality and enthusiasm, and the driving force behind Grimwades Royal Winton Pottery. The *North Staffordshire Echo* profiled him in 1907, describing him as 'quick in all his movements, restless in activity, audacious in projects, with fine imagination and generous sentiments, he is an interesting personality and an admirable ally.'

Lily Bell, who worked at Winton Potteries during the 1920s and 1930s said, "Leonard Grimwade, he was absolutely alive. He was full of it. No sooner than he'd thought anything, he was off – he was like a bottle of pop; got to be doing."

Leonard Grimwade was born in Ipswich in 1864, the youngest of nine children. Large families were then common; Leonard's father, Richard Grimwade (1816-1905), was one of 15 children, while his uncle, Edward, produced 17 children. Leonard's grandfather, William Grimwade (1782-1856), was a Suffolk man who owned Poplar Farm at Wetheringsett, some 16 miles from Ipswich. Amy Langdon, Leonard Grimwade's mother, was a woollen draper at the time of her marriage.

At 16, Leonard moved to Hanley in North Staffordshire where he worked for his uncle, Edward, as a 'dry-salter'. According to a contemporary dictionary, the term dry-salter had two definitions: a dealer in dried and salted meats, pickles and sauces, or a dealer in dye stuffs, chemical products etc. As Leonard's uncle was a chemist, it can be assumed that the boy worked with chemicals rather than pickles.

By 1880, however, he was working as a decorator and modeller in the potteries. He soon began to show signs of the restless energy and dynamism that were to characterise him in later life and, shortly before he was 21, he opened his own business as a factor, the manufacturing side being developed gradually. His first premises consisted of no more than a shed in a yard, sited between two rows of cottages but, before long, he was in a position to invite his elder brother Sidney Richard Grimwade, a potter, to join him in his venture. And so, in 1885, the firm of Grimwade Brothers was founded. Around the late 1880s, another Grimwade brother, Edward Ernest, joined the firm. He was later to represent the company's interests in Australasia, leaving England in 1905 to live in New Zealand.

In 1886, Leonard returned to Ipswich to marry Marion Cooper (1865-1925). There were three children of the marriage: a son, Charles Donovan Grimwade (1890-1971), and two daughters, Elsie (born in 1892) and Muriel (born in 1907). It appeared to have been a happy marriage. The Grimwades celebrated their silver wedding anniversary in style in 1911 when family members, colleagues and employees, (in all numbering some 900 people), filled the Victoria Hall at Hanley. The *Staffordshire Sentinel* reported that the couple had been presented with a gift from their employees of a silver rose bowl and two silver vases.

There was another reason for the celebration, the *Staffordshire Sentinel* declared. 'It was primarily a recognition by the firm of the loyalty of its employees during the rush of orders attendant upon the Coronation.'

Leonard Grimwade's reply to the presentation threw light on his early days as a manufacturer. When he wooed and won his wife all those years ago, he said, the business of Grimwades Ltd was in its infancy. The whole work of the firm was carried on in one small warehouse, and he was the warehouseman, ledger clerk, and sometimes the packer. This statement was greeted with much laughter and applause.

Marion Grimwade died in 1925 and Leonard re-married shortly afterwards. His new wife, Minnie, presented him with a baby girl, Janet, in 1927.

Charles Donovan Grimwade was to follow his father into the pottery business. He left school at 17 and worked at the Shelton laboratory in 1908, later moving to the Atlas works. When he was twenty, he was presented with a bronze medal by the County Borough of Stoke-on-Trent. The inscription reads: *Higher Education Committee. Examination in Pottery. Charles Donovan Grimwade. 2nd Place Honours Grade 1910-11.*

Shortly after taking the examination in 1912, Charles Donovan went to China where he was in charge of the Chinese Mining and Engineering Company. Based in Tongshan, North China, the works was spread over two acres and manufactured tiles and stonework piping as well as bricks. Charles Donovan was responsible for reporting on the state of affairs in clay mining, works machinery and output, as well as estimating the quantities needed, weight and cost, and time of manufacture for articles produced.

He left Tongshan in December 1915 to join the army. He left for Petrograd via the Trans-Siberian Railway, then travelled by sledge to the Swedish railway (in the Arctic winter) then on to Bergen in Norway. He reached England on January 13th 1916 and soon received a commission going first to Egypt, then Palestine, being present at the capture of Jerusalem.

After the war, he became scientific advisor to Grimwades, and was soon on the Board of Directors. He married Nora Gibson in 1920, the daughter of Arthur Gibson, who was well-known for his manufacture of teapots. The couple had one daughter, Stella Ruth.

Charles Donovan's work in China appears to have been recognised by his father, as several shape names bear reference to the oriental. The 1918 catalogue, for example, shows a **Tientsin** toilet set and a **Tongshan** vase. The war years were also commemorated in the same catalogue, with toilet ware having shape names such as **Belgium** and **Somme**.

As the silver wedding celebration showed, Leonard Grimwade was known as a kindly employer. In 1892, *The Pottery Gazette* recorded a New Year's Day party at Grimwades. 'In one of the large rooms at the new works, which had been tastefully decorated for the occasion, a sumptuous repast had been spread ... A lengthy programme of music – vocal and instrumental – readings, dancing and various games, gave pleasure to all.'

Several employees who worked at Royal Winton during the 1930s and earlier mentioned the room resembling a ballroom that was at the top of the building. "It (the ballroom) was massive. There were great wide stairs and a lovely wooden banister," one worker said. "It looked to me as though it had been a place that had had a lot of money spent on it years ago. Upstairs it was very nice. We used to practise (dancing) there in our lunch time." Another worker recalled the sprung maple floor and lamented the day it was turned into a showroom for toilet and dinner ware.

The girls entered into the spirit of Christmas at the factory. Florence Dennis remembers how they made paper decorations. "We decorated the shop with crêpe paper we bought for tuppence a roll. We made orchids on a steel knitting needle and hung them all around, all the loveliest colours. I'll never forget it. And Leonard Grimwade came in and he said, 'Fairyland! It's fairyland. Beautiful.' He walked through in his plus-fours; he was a grand old man."

At the turn of the century, business was booming and the export trade was brisk. The year 1900 saw the acquisition of the Stoke Pottery and Grimwades Ltd was established, while a new showroom was set up in London. Between 1901 and 1907, four more potteries were bought out and added to the Grimwades Group.

In 1906, Grimwades took out a full page advertisement in *The Pottery Gazette* in order to contradict 'Two Representatives of Earthenware Manufacturers in Staffordshire who have persistently published malicious statements to the effect that we are not Manufacturers, but only Decorators or Factors. We have been compelled to take out Legal Proceedings in order to prevent such innuendoes.' The statement went on: 'We are just publishing a little 'brochure' explaining the chief processes carried on in making pottery.'

The brochure was ostensibly printed to commemorate the opening of the new showrooms at Winton Pottery on October 25th 1906, but would have had a secondary purpose of squashing any further talk or rumours. The booklet, entitled *A Short Description of the Art of Potting...as carried on by Grimwades Ltd at Winton, Stoke, Elgin & Upper Hanley Potteries*, is well illustrated with scenes showing the clay presses in the slip house, the potters' shop, the 'biscuit' warehouse and so on. Some of the photographs were later used for a commemorative catalogue issued in 1913.

The company was awarded a gold medal for some of its Hygienic Patented Ware in 1911, at the Festival of Empire, Imperial Exhibition and Pageant.

King George V and Queen Mary visited the Potteries in 1913 and

Grimwades issued a catalogue commemorating the royal visit. This gave a short history of the firm as well as illustrating their ware. In addition, photographs (taken from the 1906 booklet) showed interiors of the dinner ware showroom, the toilet ware showroom, warehouses and the mould makers' shop. It also illustrated how employees carried out skills such as plate making, aerographing, gilding and enamelling.

During their visit, the royal couple toured numerous factories before attending an exhibition at the King's Hall in Stoke-on-Trent. *The Pottery Gazette* reported in their June edition that 'Grimwades had the largest individual exhibit in the whole display'.

The company were showing their new 'Jacobean' ware, a vine-leafed pattern which was a copy of early 17th century tapestry. Also featured was **Royal Hampton**, a pattern taken from old Queen Anne chintz, and 'executed in pink, black and green'. **Royal Dorset** was another new pattern and this consisted of massed roses on a black ground.

The Queen was apparently delighted to purchase a Grimwades Winton teaset in the new **Queen Mary Chintz**. She was also pleased to receive a gift of the **Mecca Foot Warmer** (a type of oval ceramic hot water bottle) in the **Jacobean** pattern. Leonard Grimwade, never one to miss a promotional opportunity, later used a full colour illustration of this in a catalogue describing the foot warmer as, 'Graciously accepted by Her Majesty the Queen'. An ornate gold and red crown decorates the head of the page.

Two days later, the exhibition was moved to Harrods' Stores in London and from there it went to the Liverpool Trades Exhibition.

The year 1920 was a year of change. Grimwades purchased a new 5-ton 'Karrier' motor lorry, costing £1,300. The company also installed gas-fired tunnel ovens which were to be 'lit-up' in September of that year. The famous *Quick-Cooker* was now being made in aluminium instead of semi-porcelain as before and a research laboratory was erected at the Victory Works (part of the Winton Works) with Charles Donovan Grimwade supervising it.

A catalogue for this period sounds a hopeful note: 'The War has so completely revolutionized industry that we embrace the opportunity which reconstruction offered for the complete reorganisation of our six factories. The introduction of new and approved methods of 'MASS PRODUCTION', whereby orders can be despatched more promptly and output can be increased, has enabled us to give greater satisfaction to customers and employees alike.'

Grimwades now employed well over a thousand workers and a Managers' Council was set up by the company to form a link between the directors and the staff in order to increase efficiency.

Further care was taken of workers. The 1920 catalogue reports that: 'A charming bungalow at Ashley Heath has, by the kindness of Mr & Mrs L.L. Grimwade, been placed at the disposal of the 'Welfare Work' and any of our workers needing a rest or country air, can have a few days there to recuperate . . . Many have been completely set up and strengthened for the duties of life at this bracing spot. Already the health of our workers has so improved that frequently it is difficult to find even 3 or 4 out of 1,500 employees who need the recreative benefits which this institution provides.'

The Ashley Heath bungalow was the site of a works outing in Easter of that year, when 85 employees sat down to tea and enjoyed sports and games on the heath.

Leonard Grimwade kept his finger on the pulse of his empire, and he travelled extensively, visiting the United States, Canada, Italy, Germany, Switzerland, Norway, Belgium, Holland, Egypt and Australia. Compelled by his restless energy to realise the value of time, he was one of the earliest motorists and drove his own car.

He was a Liberal free-trader and served on the Stoke-on-Trent County Borough Council. He was also a Justice of the Peace for Staffordshire and Secretary of the Potteries Association for the Promotion of Federation. When examined during the passing of the Federation Bill through Parliament he was asked where he lived. "I sleep in Wolstanton," came the reply, "but I live in the Potteries."

Perhaps his words make a fitting epitaph for such a man.

He died as he had lived – at top speed – in a car crash when on his way to the factory on the 26th January 1931. Accompanied by his nephew, who was in the passenger seat, Leonard Grimwade failed to avoid a bus at crossroads. He died almost instantaneously and was buried at Hartshill Cemetery.

A report in *The Pottery Gazette* stated: 'There was a big cortège, representing all sections of the local life of the Potteries, and the floral tributes were eloquent of the sense of loss which, by the passing of Mr Grimwade, the district has sustained.'

Products

Early Grimwades catalogues, dating from 1888, show a range of useful domestic items. The company concentrated mainly on toilet sets, comprising wash stand jugs, wash bowls, toothbrush vases, soap and sponge dishes, and chamber pots. They also made matching trinket sets (composed of trays, chamber or candlesticks) trinket pots, pin trays and ring stands.

As well as this they manufactured an extensive range of table ware with dinner and tea ware being produced in a variety of patterns and shapes, together with additional items such as cheese dishes, bacon dishes, biscuit boxes and sardine dishes.

More mundane products were also made, such as the *Hygienic Hospital and Nurseryware*. This ware consisted of bedpans (including one with an airtight lid for the use of typhoid patients), and urinals (*sic*) for both male and female use, children's chamber pots, slop pails, sick-feeders and ceramic hot water bottles.

For the housewife, they produced jelly and blancmange moulds, fluted pudding bowls for turning out ribbed sponge puddings, lemon squeezers, pie funnels and square pie dishes (known as bakers) of various sizes which fitted neatly into one another.

The range of patented products was both wide and ingenious. The **Paragon** coffee pot had a removable strainer, while the **Patent Tea Machine** had a valve operated infuser. The **Safety Milk Bowl** had an in-curving rim to prevent spillage when carried and the contents of the bowl were guaranteed safe from flies. 'Those who study the habits of flies', wrote *The Pottery Gazette*, 'say they would not enter the bowl by means of the curved rim – but that the slope of the spout forms a ready convenient passage of which they make good use.' Leonard Grimwade solved the problem by the addition of a patented spout cover which fitted over the spout, thus preventing any contamination. This design was awarded a Gold Medal in 1911.

The **Patent Pie Dish** was practically fireproof and a guarantee was given that the contents of the dish would not burn, due to a series of ring grooves at the bottom of the dish.

In 1909, the **Patent Quick-Cooker Bowl** was introduced and this had the virtue of doing away with un-hygienic pudding cloths tied over a bowl by having a grooved ceramic lid which could be fastened down with string. The Quick-Cooker was available in no less than five sizes.

But perhaps the most ingenious and attractive of all was the patent hygienic **Toilet 'Holdall'**. This was a large shell shaped dish which would have stood between a set of two toilet jugs and basins. The 'Holdall' was divided into five sections and held two cakes of soap, two nail brushes, and a sponge. There were also four ringed holders for toothbrushes.

In 1902, the two Climax kilns were working overtime, turning out 15000 commemorative mugs and beakers every 24 hours in preparation for the coronation of Edward VII. Grimwades claimed that at least five million mugs and beakers would be needed for the British Isles and, judging by their advertising, it would appear that the company were quite prepared to make every one of them.

Some of the prettiest toilet ware was made by Grimwades in the early 1900s, with the **Nautilus** toilet set being relief moulded in an attractive shell shape. The jug had a handle at the top instead of at the side, as was customary. 'Oh, how easily it pours!' proclaimed the advertisement.

Many chintz patterns were being produced, and Jacobean, Hampton, and Spode Chintz were all greatly admired by Her Majesty Queen Mary when, with King George V, she visited the Potteries in 1913. Matching trinket sets were available with the toilet sets, but what took the Queen's fancy was the new **Mecca Foot Warmer** or hot water bottle and, according to contemporary accounts, she was delighted to be presented with one in the *Jacobean* pattern. The foot warmer had a patent screw top, designed by Charles Donovan Grimwade, and a tasselled silk cord was tied into holes on either side of the neck for ease of carrying.

The Pottery Gazette eulogised over the toilet ware produced by Grimwades and much comment was made about the skilful modelling, the fine selection of shapes and delicate colours used.

It is sometimes thought that it was at around this period that Royal Winton adopted the prefix Royal to the Winton trade name. A press release issued some years ago by a development and promotion group wrongly asserts that the prefix was added in 1930 when the Royal couple visited the potteries. This is obviously incorrect, as the visit was in 1913, but such inaccuracies are often passed on and assumed to be true.

In actual fact, the Home Office, whose records go back to 1897, can find no trace of Grimwades applying for or receiving permission to use the word 'royal' as a prefix. And, far from the use of the title dating from 1913, a catalogue for 1896 (when the firm was still trading as Grimwade Brothers) shows a full colour illustration for *Royal Winton Ware*. This shows tea and coffee pots, cocoa jugs, beer or milk sets, cruets, egg sets, cups and saucers and pillar candlesticks made in plain colours of celadon, terracotta, ivory and beige, banded with contrasting colours of sage green, brown and turquoise blue.

However, the name Royal Winton does not appear on ware until about 1917/18 when Royal Winton Ware was produced (See Backstamp No. 2). It did not appear again, however, either in advertising or in catalogues, until about 1929, when Grimwades took out a full page advertisement in *The Pottery Gazette* introducing their new **Octron** vegetable dish made in Royal Winton Ivory. However, examples of *Marguerite* chintz, made in 1928, show the Royal Winton backstamp used in the familiar Art Deco style.

Leonard Grimwade ensured maximum publicity for his company. He advertised widely in the trade papers, invited journalists to inspect the new showrooms as they were opened, and exhibited at trade fairs. His strategy worked and *The North Staffordshire Echo* commented that Mr Grimwade had 'succeeded in establishing one of the largest businesses in the Potteries' with 'agencies or branches all over the world and is a marvel of organisation and energy.'

The first 'novelty' ware appeared around 1907 with the introduction of nursery ware decorated with illustrated quotations from nursery rhymes, while **Brownies** 'quaint and amusing figures' adorned heraldic china. World War I saw the introduction of **Patriotic Ware**, with each article stamped 'Made by the girls of Staffordshire during the Great War, when the Boys were in the trenches fighting for Liberty and Civilization'. The **Bairnsfather Souvenir Ware** was also made at this time and carried 'photographic reproductions of Captain Bairnsfather's inimitable Cartoons of the Great War'.

In 1922, another range of nursery ware, this time featuring **Black Cats** appeared, together with **Imps** and an updated version of **Brownies**. These were followed in 1925 by **Aesop's Fables, Robinson Crusoe, Old Country Nursery Rhymes, Bubbles** and **Piggies**.

Art and novelty wares were not neglected, either, and these ranged from tobacco jars, in scenic designs or old chintz patterns, to jardinieres, similarly decorated.

Floating bowls (large shallow bowls, sometimes on a pedestal, having an in-curving rim) were made in 1925, using the new *Byzanta* lustre in rich colours of tangerine, powder blue, maroon (wine red), cyclamen, yellow and turquoise. Pierced flower blocks supported smaller flowers, while 'Floweraids', either in the shape of perching birds on trees or of tree trunks with stumpy branches, were available to support larger blooms. Purchasers could also buy 'rim birds' to perch on the side of the bowl.

The **Byzanta** lustre ware proved popular and the range was expanded to take in vases of every shape and size, fruit bowls, jardinieres, toilet ware and some table ware. It was reintroduced in 1937. *The Pottery Gazette* reported in October of that year: 'A new series of ornamental ware has been produced, inspired by the old and thoroughly successful 'Byzanta' ware. The colours, which are underglaze, are rich and intensive, such as ruby and mazarine blue, and the patternings are strongly traced in gold by hand.'

Grimwades introduced their new chintz ware in 1928, and this was manufactured on a large scale between the late 1920s and early 1950s. The company also offered new designs and shapes in basic tea and dinner ware.

They pioneered several new ranges of relief-modelled ware in 1933. **Primula** based on the flower and **Regina**, based on the water lily, were made by Rubian Art, with **Gera** (geranium) being made by Royal Winton in 1935. **Lakeland, Chanticleer** and **Rooster** (both cockerel designs), **Pixie, Beehive**, and others – all fashioned in the shapes of teapots, jugs, biscuit boxes, cheese dishes, cruets, sugar sifters and wall plates – followed from 1936 onwards.

Cottages were featured in **Old Cottage Ware** with **Ye Olde Inne**, **Anne Hathaway's Cottage** and **Old Mill** being introduced in 1934 and 1935, and items similar to those previously listed were manufactured.

During World War II, an effort was made by the potteries to increase export sales and this drive was spearheaded by Gordon Forsyth, the former principal of the Burslem School of Art, and a designer of considerable ability. He recruited successful designers such as Mabel Leigh, Eric Tunstall, Norma Smallwood and Billy Grindy and the Winton Potteries set up two studios for their use. Mabel Leigh, who had done such excellent work for Shorter, worked there between 1939 and 1945, and produced many strikingly lovely lustred patterns in strong, yet subtle colours. Much of her work was never fully exploited, the right market seemingly never being found.

Gordon Forsyth, known affectionately as 'Fuzzy', also worked with lustres at Grimwades, using silver and copper lustres to achieve dramatic abstract patterns and designs reminiscent of those produced for Pilkington's Royal Lancastrian ware with rampant dragons and leaping deer. He also experimented with scraffito patterns.

Norma Smallwood was best known for her tapestry designs, while Billy Grindy modelled the Royal Winton character jugs. These were based on wartime personalities, such as George VI, Winston Churchill, Uncle Sam, General McArthur and others. He was later to model similar items for Sylvac, eventually moving to Thomas C. Wild's factory where he designed the Montreaux shape for the Royal Albert 'Country Roses' pattern.

In April 1940 *The Pottery Gazette* praised the new range of **Rosebud** ware. This was made in plain underglaze colours of pink, green, cream and yellow. Interest was added by the roses, modelled in relief and hand painted, which were used to adorn the handles and knobs on tea ware, or which were strategically incorporated on dishes and plates, etc. Other flowers were added to the range, such as petunias, honey lilies, pansies, briar (roses), fuchsias and tea roses.

After the War, Polish refugees were employed by Grimwades at the Elgin factory. The hand painted ware they produced was in the style of paintings by the famous still-life painter, William Hunt, and pieces can be found with anemones superbly depicted.

In the 1950s, in an effort to combat the recession that had succeeded the post-war boom, and which had destroyed the chintz market, Royal Winton produced a range of items in gold and silver lustre. Only the best quality materials were used, the silver lustres closely resembled silver plate (the silver effect being achieved by the use of platinum), while the gold lustres had a deep, rich colour. Coloured lustre ware was again produced in the 1950s/1960s, but this was a pale imitation of the rich lustres that had been made in former years. Unfortunately, the take-over by Howard Potteries in 1964 proved to be the death-knell of the exciting, innovative designs that had been a feature for over 70 years.

Chintz Ware

The term 'chintz' applies to the tightly grouped, small floral patterns which are reminiscent of chintz fabrics, for example, **Marguerite** and **Balmoral**. Sheet transfer printed patterns are not necessarily floral but cover the whole piece with an 'allover' design, such as **Queen Anne** or **Paisley**. Both chintz and sheet pattern wares are popular with collectors today.

Grimwades first introduced chintz patterns in 1913, with ware decorated in **Hampton** Chintz, **Spode** Chintz, **Ribbon** Chintz and the **Jacobean** pattern. These were sheet transfer printed patterns, the flowers being large or widely spaced. The first closely packed sheet pattern was used in 1923 when **Paisley** was made. In 1928, the chintz ware that is collected today made its first appearance with the **Marguerite** pattern. This was based on the design of a cushion cover that Minnie Grimwade (Leonard Grimwade's second wife) was embroidering at the time.

In 1931, **Delphinium** chintz was produced, and that was followed in 1932 by **Summertime**.

It would appear, from regular reports in *The Pottery Gazette*, that Royal Winton was the leader in the field of chintz ware, easily outstripping manufacturers such as James Kent, Crown Ducal, W.R. Midwinter, and Elijah Cotton who made Nelson Ware.

Leonard Grimwade had bought a large number of shares in the Chromo Transfer and Potters' Supply Co Ltd in 1908 and he was able to translate his ideas for patterns quickly into the reality of transfer printed sheets. He was enthusiastic about the new chintz and, according to Lily Bell who worked at Winton Potteries at the time, he 'would rush out of his office if he saw a girl with a nice overall (a type of wrap-around pinafore) on, like a chintzy pattern, and get her on one side and ask her to leave her overall behind (when she went home) and get someone to take a drawing of it. It'd be a pattern in no time.'

As Leonard Grimwade died in 1931, a great many patterns must already have been in the production pipeline at the time of his death.

The two men who actually put the new patterns down on paper were Mr E.E. Parry, Art Director, and Gilbert Sergeant, Decorating Manager. Between them, they produced innumerable patterns. Florence Dennis, who was also employed by Grimwades during that period recalled, 'There were umpteen patterns in chintz – and Bert Sergeant did quite a lot of designing.'

Chintz patterns were applied by means of a lithographic process. First of all, the biscuit (unglazed) ware was dipped into a transparent liquid glaze and then allowed to dry for 24 hours before being fired. The backstamp was rubber stamped on to the ware before glazing, the glaze being transparent. Once dry the ware was fired in a kiln, allowed to cool and then collected by the girls who were to do the decorating.

The transfer sheets were supplied by the Chromo-Transfer and Potters' Supply Co Ltd who were based at the Winton Potteries. Albert Stevenson, who worked at Winton Potteries for over 30 years said, "The sheets of transfers were hung on a line to dry, rather like washing. The girls, called transferrers or lithographers would cut off the required amount needed and take it back to their bench."

Lithographing was hard work. Glue, (called *size*) was brushed on to the ware by means of a camel hair brush and left to become tacky. Glazed ware, rather than biscuit, was used for chintz as this gave the finished article brighter colours. Unfortunately, this brightness was sometimes at the cost of the durability of the pattern. The lithographer would then cut the sheet of transfer to fit the object as nearly as possible, using a pair of long pointed scissors. Florence Dennis commented, "It was very intricate. We didn't have knives like we had later, where you could nick around the spout of the teapot, for example. But it was very interesting, and I loved it. The harder the pattern, the better I liked it, because I've done nothing else all my life, only lithograph."

The cut pieces of transfer were pressed onto the sized ware. Mrs Dennis explained, "Then I fetched a pot of boiling water from the geyser and took it to the bench. You rubbed with a hard sponge, then a soft one, to take the paper off (leaving the transfer printed pattern adhering to the sized surface). Then you went over it with a clean rag."

To avoid an obvious join, the flowers were often cut into one another, although some badly mis-matched work can be found. Seams and creases were frowned upon and mistakes were not tolerated.

The pattern name was also put on at this stage and the girls often marked their work with a small gilded or painted mark. These marks were put on to the base of the piece, so that any poor or unacceptable work could be traced to the culprit. Sybil Stevenson, for example, used three small dots set in a triangle, rather like two eyes and a nose, to mark her work.

If the work was so bad that even touching up by a skilled paintress was impossible, then the lithographer responsible had to remove the transfer. This was done by soaking the piece in a bucket of soda water, then laboriously scraping off the transfer. As the girls were paid on a piece work basis for finished work, their mistakes could cost them dearly.

Girls were trained initially to decorate a cup (both inside and out) and a saucer, and the completed article had to be passed by an inspector to prove the girl's worth as a lithographer.

After adding any gilding necessary to the piece, it was again fired in the kiln in order to fuse the colours into the glaze and so make them almost permanent. The colours of prefired pieces were 'dull but, after firing, they came up nice and bright.'

Some of the chintz designs were reserved exclusively for the Winton

Potteries, but a few were sold to other pottery manufacturers, especially during the 1950s. **Rose Violet** (Rose du Barry) for example, has been seen on ware produced by several other companies; however, the piece illustrated on page 68 bears the Royal Winton backstamp. **Paisley**, too, was used by others and has been seen in both the rust and blue colourway.

During World War II, the decorating of white ware was forbidden by the government and only practical ware was manufactured. Some unscrupulous dealers would buy up the seconds, then approach factory girls, paying them good money to decorate a teaset or other items in chintz.

One worker admitted, "I did the black market work. This bloke came to the door and asked me to do him 10 china tea sets – he had a couple of sheets of litho, maybe two or three sheets. And I said 'Yes, I'll get you something out of these'."

She was paid half a crown (12½ pence) per teaset which she thought was marvellous. "We had bad times in the potteries then," she said. "So I did these tea sets and it got a bit more, a bit too much. I realised something was going on. It was in the War, you see."

After the post-war boom, the pottery trade went into recession and, by the early to mid-1950s, chintz ware was no longer being produced. The company was left with a stock of lithographed sheets which were sold on to other manufacturers, and consequently, collectors may find pieces with Royal Winton transfers on products from other potteries.

What Comes Next?

Once collectors have discovered a factory and read its history, they are often quite keen to collect further products. There is already growing interest in the Royal Winton relief moulded ware, such as *Gera*, *Lakeland*, *Beehive*, *Pixie* and the cockerel series *Chanticleer*. The cottage ware, made by both Royal Winton and Rubian Art (a subsidiary of Royal Winton) offers a wide range of collectable pieces, also.

All the above ranges were made in 'fancies' and items can be found such as teapots, hot water jugs, cream and sugar sets, marmalade and jam pots with covers, sugar sifters, cheese dishes, cruets, toast racks, covered butter dishes, mint boats and stands and dessert plates (some with musical stands). Some ranges include biscuit boxes, vases (all sizes), baskets (various sizes) and wall clocks.

Rubian Art also produced tea ware in relief moulded flower patterns; such as *Primula* and *Regina* and these, too, are collectable. Apart from the tea ware, collectors can find cake comports, salad bowls, sugar sifters, triple dishes, 4-place egg sets, dessert and sandwich sets.

The *Rosebud* range with its plain colours and rose decoration was made in complete contrast to the relief moulded ware and is extremely popular. Using underglaze air-blown ground colours of pink, yellow, green and cream, items had moulded handles and knobs brush-painted in natural colours. The new design was made as table ware, and further patterns, apart from Rosebud, include *Petunia*, *Honey Lily*, *Pansy*, *Briar*, *Fuchsia* and *Rose*.

Apart from table ware, some of the patterns can be found as bedside sets, tennis sets, butter trays and knifes (often boxed), jam dishes and spoons (again, boxed) watercress dishes, salad bowls and servers, triple trays, chocolate comports, wall pockets and vases, trinket sets and chamber sticks.

The range of *Byzanta* ware, first introduced in 1925 and reintroduced in 1937, proved popular with buyers at the time and is just as popular today. Made in rich lustred colours of both pale and deep blue, orange, pale green, wine red and cream, the ware was mainly ornamental. Large and small bowls, vases in all sizes, wall pockets and so on, can be found, with the occasional teapot or sandwich set also being available. The later lustred ware, produced after the company was taken over by Howards, was made in paler colours and is less dramatic in appearance.

The wartime character jugs are less frequently seen than the ware mentioned above but are, nevertheless, eagerly sought after. Modelled by Billy Grinder, and made in various sizes, they include personalities such as George VI, Winston Churchill, Field Marshal Wavell, Field Marshal Smuts, General McArthur and an archetypal Uncle Sam, who rather resembles Abraham Lincoln. President Franklin D. Roosevelt was portrayed as a head only, the jug having a scroll handle.

A particularly striking character jug was modelled after an Indian Chief and is shown wearing a large feathered head dress.

Musical jugs were first made for the coronation of George VI in 1937. Intended for use as beer or cider tankards, they could be supplied with or without musical fittings. Tunes played were 'God Save the King' or 'Here's A Health Unto His Majesty'.

Other musical jugs followed and were portrayed in scenic fashion with detailed handles, such as 'Balmoral Castle' with its Stuart tartan. Musical chromed stands for cake comports were also made.

Hopefully, this book will enlighten collectors to the wider range of collectable pottery made by Grimwades – it was certainly a far bigger concern than many people realise.

Patterns

When referring to chintz ware, it is generally the tightly packed floral designs that is meant by the term. However, it can sometimes be difficult to draw a distinct line between chintz, sheet transfer patterns and all-over patterns. Therefore for ease of reference, all patterns, whether chintz, sheet transfer, or all-over design, have been included in the following list.

Some sheet patterns, such as Fernese and 'Paisley', pre-date the first real chintz pattern, Marguerite, but these have been included as they, too, are collectable.

Another difficulty that faces the collector is the fact that some of the patterns are un-named. For ease of reference, these patterns have been given identifying names which can be seen written in quotes, such as 'Blue Tulip', 'Exotic Bird' and 'Rose Spray'.

An attempt has been made to describe and identify the flowers that make up the patterns, although botanical accuracy cannot be guaranteed as many of the flowers have been vaguely drawn and are unidentifiable. However, some are surprisingly accurately drawn and botanically correct, such as the *Eryngium Maritimum*, commonly known as *Sea Holly*, which can be seen on Fireglow (Black).

It would appear that the pattern names fall into three categories: girls' names, flowers or floral subjects, and place names. Where applicable, place names and locations have been identified.

Dates and shapes are mentioned only if they can be verified. The information has been taken from various Grimwades catalogues and advertising fly sheets, and from the pages of the *The Pottery Gazette*. No date is given unless it can established with an exact reference. Nevertheless, it is clear that the majority of the better chintz patterns were created and produced between the years 1932 and 1939.

This was a period of explosive output and gained the company a reputation for excellence. *The Pottery Gazette* reports in 1937, 'Grimwades Ltd have a reputation, of course, for chintz patterns. In this connection we have heard them referred to as an acknowledged pre-eminent house. Dealers in search of an allover pattern can, therefore, approach the Winton Potteries with confidence that they will find what they are requiring.'

Anemone (picture page 50)
Backstamp 4 with the words 'Hand Painted' in script, transfer printed in dark blue, a greeny blue, and mid-blue.
The flowers in this design represent the spring flowering anemone, also known as the Windflower and which is related to the Wood Anemone.
This is a transfer-printed pattern with a hand painted infill on the

flowers. It can be found in two colourways. The first has hand-painted creamy anemones which have pale to deep orange centres. These are set against well defined green leaves and are accompanied by pale lavender Michaelmas daisies, with small flower heads enamelled in turquoise blue. The ground colour is a dark almost navy blue.

The second colourway has vivid yellow hand-painted anemones with red enamelled centres. The Michaelmas daisies are a muted pink, and are set against pale green leaves on a mid-blue ground. There is no enamelling on the small flower heads apart from a spot of red in the centres.

Balmoral (picture page 50)
Backstamp 4, 8
Densely packed flowers and leaves are shown against a black ground. Some of the flowers are unidentifiable, but there are pink roses, shaded pink anemones, pale pink irises, white daisies with yellow centres, several meadow flowers, sprays of blue flower heads, and sprays of orange and yellow budding flower heads.

The name refers to the castle in Scotland.

Bedale (picture page 50)
Backstamp 4
This is an alternative colourway to Summertime, the second pattern issued by Royal Winton. The roses on Bedale are yellow instead of pink, and the smaller briar roses are shown as pink and not yellow. However, the white daisies and bluebells remain the same in both patterns.

The name refers to a town in Yorkshire.

Beeston (picture page 50)
Backstamp 4
A dramatic rendering of pink and yellow roses accompanied by green leaves set against a black ground. The quality of transfer printing is extremely high and pieces have an attractive glossy finish. The pattern was used on angular Art Deco shapes as well as those of a more traditional nature.

The name refers to towns in Cheshire, Norfolk, Bedfordshire, Nottingham and West Yorkshire.

'Birds and Tulips' (picture page 51)
Backstamp GRIMWADES ROYAL WINTON IVORY ENGLAND transfer printed in green.
A very stylised Art Deco pattern showing birds printed in pink, red and blue perched on branches amongst sprays of pink and yellow tulips, bunches of yellow and red seeds and grey and green leaves. The other

flowers in red, pink, yellow and dark blue are extremely stylised and botanically unrecognisable. The white ground is stippled with blue dots.

'Blue Anemone' – now known to be Chintz (picture page 51)
Backstamp 4
The flowers in this pattern are autumn flowering anemones, unlike those in the Anemone pattern which are spring flowering Windflowers. The blooms are in shades of red and blue and there are splashes of green leaves. The remaining foliage is blue and there is no ground colour to be seen.

'Blue Jade' (picture page 51)
Backstamp 4
The name refers to the sprays of turquoise blue flowers which appear to be a dwarf variety of the delphinium known as Blue Jade. The other blossoms in the pattern are possibly briar or rambling roses and are in shades of pink and blue. A few leaves are additionally hand-painted in gold. The background colour is a smudgy blue on white.

'Blue Tulip' (picture page 51)
Backstamp GRIMWADES ROYAL WINTON IVORY ENGLAND transfer printed in green.
Deep blue tulips with paler shading and outlined in yellow are set against yellow leaves. Smaller flowers are also in yellow, accentuated by grey leaves and occasional branches of deep blue leaves. The ground colour is black.

Cheadle (picture page 52)
Backstamp 4, 8
Registration numbers for Canada 1951 and USA 166273.
Summer flowers defy recognition in this pattern. There are, what appear to be, white and yellow briar roses set against green rose leaves, with additional blue harebells, and small yellow and cerise flower heads. These are all set against a creamy white ground.

    The name refers to towns in Staffordshire and Greater Manchester in Lancashire.

Chelsea (picture page 52)
Backstamp 4
Registration numbers for Canada 1952.
A striking pattern predominantly featuring large pink roses and white briar roses with blue centres. These are accompanied by sprays of

orange flowers, pale blue buds and green leaves, set against a black ground. The pattern is easily confused with Esther on smaller pieces.
Name refers to an area in London.

Chintz – see 'Blue Anemone'

Clevedon 1934 (picture page 53)
Backstamp 4
Branching sprays of pink and yellow roses accompanied by green leaves dominate this pattern, with smaller daisy-like flowers in yellow, white and blue giving added colour. The background is cream, stippled with tiny yellow dots, giving the appearance of a pale yellow ground. There is a deep pink or cerise edging to the ware. On some examples of Clevedon, the white flowers are replaced by those of a deep blue.
Clevedon offers an alternative colourway to the Cranstone pattern. The colours of the flowers are the same, except that the white flowers on Clevedon are blue in Cranstone and the stippling is of a vivid green.
The pattern was recommended to the trade by *The Pottery Gazette* in January 1934.
Name refers to a town at the mouth of the Severn near Bristol, Avon.

Clyde (picture page 53)
Pattern number possibly 5637
Backstamp 4
This pattern was made in two colourways, both on a white ground. Pale apricot and yellow primroses are dotted singly, accompanied by green leaves. Alternatively, the flowers are pink and yellow set against brown leaves.
Name refers to the river and area near Glasgow in Scotland.

Cotswold (picture page 53)
Backstamp 8, 9
Registration numbers for Canada 1952 and Australia 29774.
Apple blossom buds and harebells trim a central bouquet of unidentified flowers in pink, yellow and blue. A spray of pink roses is matched with smaller flowers in a pale rust. The ground colour is a very clear white.
Name refers to a range of English hills.

Cranstone 1934 (picture page 54)
Backstamp 4
Branching sprays of pink roses accompanied by green leaves dominate this pattern, with blue and yellow daisy-like flowers giving

added colour. The ground colour is white, accentuated by vivid green dots.

Cranstone is an alternative colourway to Clevedon. The flowers are of identical colouring but the stippled background dots are green in Cranstone, yellow in Clevedon.

Again, like Clevedon, this pattern was recommended to the trade by the *The Pottery Gazette* in January 1934, when it was mis-spelled as Cranston. It was again mentioned, this time correctly spelled, in April 1935, in a report on the exhibition at Olympia. 'Good business was done with the new relief-modelled tablewares, and the 'Pelham' and 'Cranstone' chintz patterns were also very well received – more particularly so, perhaps, because the Queen (Her Majesty, Queen Mary) purchased both of these patterns.'

Origin of name unknown

Crocus (Black) 1939 (picture page 54)
Backstamp 4. Also marked GRIMWADES MADE IN ENGLAND transfer printed in green.
Bunches of yellow and blue crocuses, together with sprays of pink and blue flowers, are set against a black ground. The pattern is identical to White Crocus apart from the ground colour.

Items in Crocus were exhibited at Olympia in 1939 and the Royal Winton stand was visited by Her Majesty Queen Mary, the Duke of Kent and the Princess Royal. The Royal party bought many pieces of ware including Crocus.

Crocus (White) 1939 (picture page 54)
Backstamp 8
Bunches of yellow and blue crocuses, accompanied by sprays of pink and blue flowers, are set against a white ground. The pattern is identical to Black Crocus (above) apart from the ground colour.

Items in Crocus were exhibited at Olympia in 1939 and the Royal Winton stand was visited by Her Majesty Queen Mary, the Duke of Kent and the Princess Royal. The Royal party bought many pieces of ware including Crocus.

Cromer (picture page 54)
Backstamp 4
Registration numbers for Australia 15540
A slightly more unusual pattern with widely spaced bouquets of pink roses and yellow, pink and blue flower heads, small daffodils and pendulous pink blooms (Dicentra) set against a barred black ground.

The name refers to a town in Norfolk.

Daffodil 1939

The Daffodil pattern was mentioned in *The Pottery Gazette* in April 1939. However, examples recently seen bear only sprays of flowers, therefore not a chintz pattern.

Delphinium Chintz 1931 (picture page 55)

Pattern number 9889.
Backstamp GRIMWADES ROYAL WINTON IVORY
The Delphinium flower was first used in 1930 on Savoy shaped table ware made in Royal Winton Ivory, where sprays of the flower were widely set against a cream/white ground. The pattern was also used on toilet ware of the Savoy shape.

It appeared as a densely packed chintz pattern in 1931 and it is likely that it was the third chintz pattern issued by Grimwades. The full page advertisement in *The Pottery Gazette* in September 1932 details it as, 'An attractive Royal Winton adaptation of a popular Summer Flower.'

Although it featured in advertising before Summertime, it is clear from the written copy in *The Pottery Gazette* that Summertime was the second pattern issued.

According to the advertisement, articles supplied were tea and coffee sets, sandwich and fruit sets, cheeses, cake plates, egg sets, cruet sets, salad bowls, marmalade jars, sugars and creams, sweet dishes, footed sweets (also known as bon bon dishes), celery trays, jugs (all sizes and various shapes), teapots (all sizes and various shapes), and teapot stands.

The arching sprays of delphiniums are seen in cerise, mid-blue and dark blue and are accompanied by green leaves. The ground colour is white.

Shapes made in this pattern include a Duval jug, a Globe jug, a Fife sandwich tray, an octagonal tea plate, a footed sweet dish, a King cup and saucer and a Countess tea pot.

Dorset (picture page 55)

Backstamp 9
This is a sheet transfer pattern showing yellow petunias, shading from pale to darker hues, with pink centres and set against a white ground almost hidden by swirling pink flowers and tiny pink leaves.

Name refers to a county in Southern England.

Eleanor (picture page 55)

Backstamp 8
The light and pretty design consists of a sprigged pattern of roses, together with various accompanying flowers in pink, yellow, blue and

white. The gaps between the sprigs of flowers are interspersed with tiny stylised flower heads. The ground colour is white.

English Rose (picture page 55)
Backstamp 8
Registration numbers for Canada 1951
One of the more delicate chintz patterns. The pale pink roses are accompanied by even paler blue flowers, with green and yellow leaves set against a creamy yellow ground.

At first glance, this pattern might be confused with that of June Roses, but close examination will reveal the differences between the two. In addition, English Rose has gilding on the rim, whereas the edging of June Roses is silvered.

Estelle (picture page 56)
Backstamp 8
Registration numbers for Canada 1952. Australia 29775
Sprays of flat pink, yellow and pale lavender flowers are accompanied by apple blossom buds and green leaves set against a cream ground. The pattern is light and airy.

Esther (picture page 56)
Backstamp 4
Registration numbers for Canada 1952
A dramatic and vivid pattern. Deep pink roses, Crane's Bill (Geranium) flowers, yellow daisies and buttercups and small blue flower heads are seen against a glossy black ground. It can easily be confused with Chelsea on smaller pieces.

Evesham (picture page 56)
Backstamp 8
Registration numbers for Canada 1951, Australia 29099, New Zealand 6484, USA 166274.
An aptly named pattern, referring as it does to the rich and bountiful orchards of the Vale of Evesham.

The pattern depicts various groups of fruit: apples, pears oranges, plums, cherries, grapes, strawberries, pomegranates and figs, all set against a cream ground. The effect is one of warm autumn colours and is very pleasing.

Name refers to the Vale of Evesham situated in Glocuestershire and Worcestershire.

'Exotic Bird' (picture page 56)
Pattern number 301262
Backstamp GRIMWADES ROYAL WINTON IVORY transfer printed in green.
Brightly coloured pheasant-like birds perch on flowering branches. The birds are in colours of yellow, turquoise and warm red. The chrysanthemum-style flowers are in the same colours with leaves in turquoise and pale brown. The ground colour is cream.

Fernese 1925 (picture page 57)
Pattern number 8786
Backstamp 4
This sheet transfer printed design was advertised by Grimwades in 1925 and was originally called Fernese Diaper ware, having a triangular motif edging the wares. The ferns and butterflies were shown in white against a blue ground and the edging was in black and gold. Later Fernese ware can be seen without the diaper border and with the butterflies coloured in shades of yellow, pink and blue, apricot, with a large butterfly having red, turquoise and yellow wings. The ground colour has deepened to a mid-blue.

Fireglow (Black) (picture page 57)
Backstamp 8
This is a pattern of dramatic orange pod-like flowers (identified as Montbretia) combined with a blue flower with holly-like leaves (Eryngium Maritimum – common name Sea Holly). In addition, starry white flowers with green leaves curling in tendrils are set against a black ground.

It is totally unlike the white Fireglow pattern listed below. However, several pieces of both patterns – all bearing backstamps with the pattern name of 'Fireglow' – have confirmed the existence of two Fireglow patterns, each one entirely different to the other.

Fireglow (White) (picture page 57)
Backstamp 4
In complete contrast to the Fireglow (Black) above, this pattern has a very spring-like air to it. It features bunches of pink roses and flat yellow flowers, together with sprays of daffodils, blue bell-like flowers (possibly Scilla) and pink pendulous flowers (Dicentra). These bouquets are set against a white background outlined with grey pebbles or bubbles.

Floral Feast (picture page 57)
Backstamp 4
Widely spaced bunches of primula-like flowers feature in a rich blue,

pale pink, yellow and orange. There are additional twiggy sprays of blossom, small daisies and green leaves all set against a creamy ground. Despite the brightness of individual colouring, the whole presents a rather pale and delicate appearance.

Florence (picture page 58)
Backstamp 4, 8
Registration numbers for Canada 1953
The vivid pink of carnations draws the eye to this pattern. Also featured are cream carnations and Amaryllis belladonna flowers (sometimes known as the Belladonna Lily) in a creamy yellow, plus a myriad of small blue and pink flowers which almost conceal the black ground. The colours are vivid and the transfer printing is excellent.

Florette 1930 (picture page 59)
Pattern number 9594
This was advertised in a Grimwades catalogue for 1930 and is a sheet transfer pattern rather than a tight chintz. The stylised roses can be seen in pink and yellow with a 'halo' of mid-blue. The leaves are a reddish brown and are set against a white ground.

According to the Grimwades catalogue, the ware was made in the following shapes: Greek coffee pot, Duval jug (3 sizes), Octron sweet, Globe jug (4 sizes), Rex cheese dish (3 sizes), Elite and Countess teapots, Dane bowl, Lotus honey jar, Stafford fruit, Crown bowl, Fife sandwich tray, 5" octagonal plate, King tea cup and saucer, and an Imperial coffee cup and saucer.

'Gold Leaves' (picture page 58)
Backstamp 8 (in gold)
A highly gilded all-over pattern of tiny gold leaves interspersed with small flat flower heads enamelled in turquoise and yellow. Ground colours were of either cream or green.

Hazel (picture page 58)
Backstamp 4
The clear crisp colours of this pattern are enhanced by the mottled black ground. A large bouquet of flowers, consisting of pink and yellow roses, yellow daffodils and white narcissi, is edged by lilac tulips and purple wisteria. The pattern is interspersed with delicate green leaves. The same pattern, on different ground colours, features in both Spring and Welbeck but, in Hazel, the tulips are less well defined and the wisteria almost indistinguishable, so giving roses priority as a motif.

'Jacobinia' (picture page 60)
Pattern number possibly 4547
Backstamp 4

This has been named after the drooping, pendulous flower identified as Jacobinia pauciflora, sometimes also known as Justicia, and the ware can be seen in three colourways. Items having a white ground have the Jacobinia in pink, shading to yellow at the tips. The pattern also includes large yellow roses, pink tulip-like blossoms, pink bell flowers, yellow and pink convolvulus and several starry flowers in white, outlined with purple and yellow. The leaves are green and the background is composed of grey leaves.

In the blue ground colourway, the Jacobinia is pale yellow, the roses are pale lavender and the chrysanthemum-like flower is in shades of pink. The background leaves are entirely blue.

Jacobinia is also available in a green colourway. The roses are shaded yellow and pink, the convolvulus is blue, with the Jacobinia flower in pink shading to cream. The leaves are tan against a background of mid-green leaves.

'Japan' (picture page 60)
Backstamp: None

This may or may not be Royal Winton. The transfer printed pattern is identical to that of Hazel, Spring and Welbeck, except that it is printed on a deep blue ground, and the shape illustrated is Ascot, which is a known Royal Winton shape. However, there is no backstamp apart from the word JAPAN (without quotes) in upper case letters and transfer printed in red. This type of mark often appears on ceramics made in Japan.

Royal Winton frequently sold white undecorated ware to other factories, and some of their transfer printed patterns have been seen on ware issued by other manufacturers. However, the ceramic body of the jug illustrated has a different 'feel' to it compared with a Royal Winton jug of the same shape. The pattern has also been badly applied, with several crease marks.

No other examples of 'Japan', bearing the Grimwades Royal Winton backstamp, have yet come to light.

Joyce-Lynn (picture page 60)
Backstamp 8

Cerise anemones and bright blue convolvulus, together with yellow daisies having ragged petals, are set against a lush background of green leaves. There is no ground colour visible.

Julia (picture page 60)
Backstamp 4, 8
The apparently green background to this pattern is formed from tiny white flowers outlined in green. The flowers that feature predominantly are cerise, yellow and pale pink tea roses decorated with green leaves. There are additional sprays of small blue flower heads and deep pink briar roses.

June Festival (picture page 61)
Backstamp 8 (plain version) and Backstamp 9 (coloured version).
This pattern appears identical to Peony but is transfer printed in a different colourway. The ground colour is wine or maroon and the white peony flowers are shaded in the same colour. The example showing coloured flowers would appear to be hand painted. The flowers are shaded in colours of yellow, blue and lavender, enhanced by green leaves.

June Roses (picture page 61)
Backstamp 4. Also found with only the words MADE IN with the word ENGLAND curved below, transfer printed in green (See Backstamp 5).
It can be quite easy to confuse this pattern with that of English Rose, although, when compared side by side, the two are quite easily distinguishable from each other. The colour in June Roses is a touch more definite and, in addition to the sprays of pink roses, June Roses also has sprays of un-opened rosebuds and sprigs of wisteria. Both backgrounds are of a creamy yellow colour. The rim decoration on June Roses is silvered.

Kew (picture page 61)
Backstamp 4, 8
A rather confusing mixture of summer flowers combine to create a very pretty pattern. Pink roses nudge pink, yellow and blue daises, and overlook pink and deep blue cornflowers. There are also some rather strange-looking dahlia-like flowers which have alternating petals of orange and white. All are set on a cream ground.

There is also possibly a blue colourway of Kew; the flowers are the same colours as above, but the ground colour is pale blue. There could be several reasons for this. It could be that the unglazed biscuit was blue rather than white, or maybe the transfer printing process became discoloured in the kiln; it may even have been a trial piece. It is possible that the mystery will never be solved as no other blue pieces have yet been reported.

The name refers to an area in London.

Kinver 1934 (picture page 61)
Backstamp 4
The pattern consists basically of two sprays or bouquets of flowers. One features roses in pink and a deep improbable blue, yellow tulips with cerise tips, pink chrysanthemums and dark blue convolvulus. The other spray also has pink roses and dark blue convolvulus plus pink daisies, bright blue flower heads and a large pink daffodil with a yellow trumpet. All these flourish against a stippled yellow ground.

Kinver was recommended to trade buyers by *The Pottery Gazette* in January 1934.

The name refers to a town near Stourbridge.

Majestic (picture page 62)
Backstamp 4
A striking pattern of pale cerise anemones and vivid blue carnations, accompanied by green and ochre leaves and set against a black ground.

This is an alternative colourway of the pattern Royalty which appeared in 1936. The flowers in Royalty are deeper in colour and are set against a pale yellow ground.

Marguerite 1928 (picture page 62 and 63)
Pattern number 9467.
Backstamp 4, 11
Registration numbers for Canada 1951.
The first time this name was used by Grimwades for a pattern was in 1892 when the company was still trading as Grimwade Bros. The pattern was described as having widely spaced flowers picked out in red and pale blue, and finished with gold 'clouds'.

However, the chintz pattern Marguerite, with its pattern of white daisies, yellow and cerise flowers and sprays of bluebells set against a beige ground, made its appearance in 1928. It was used in two ways on toilet ware of the Octron shape. Pattern number 9609 had wide panels of Marguerite chintz alternating with sections of plain colour and the toilet sets were available in colours of blue, pink or old gold. Pattern number 9467 was also used on toilet sets which were available in an all-over chintz design with the rim of the ware edged in dark blue.

Leonard Grimwade's youngest daughter, Janet, was told that the design was taken from a cushion cover being embroidered by her mother.

The new chintz design – the forerunner of so many – was to prove an instant success for the company and was subsequently used on table ware. *The Pottery Gazette* maintained, in their issue for November 1929, that 'the theme (of the design) is reminiscent of the charm of the countryside, the shapes being new and unquestioningly appealing'.

They also recommended the ware as being 'eminently suitable for the Christmas trade.'.

Early shapes in Marguerite include Elite teapots, Duval and Globe jugs (both in 3 sizes), Greek coffee pots, King tea cups, Hurstmere sugar bowls, Winton cream jugs (in 5 sizes), Vera cream jugs, Stafford fruit bowls and long trays, Rex cheese dishes, large Crown bowls, and Orleans sandwich trays and plates.

Some Marguerite tableware was also made by Atlas China while under the Grimwades' ownership.

Marion (picture page 62)
Backstamp 8
Registration numbers for Canada 1951
A delicate pattern in pastel colours. The flowers appear to be white Amaryllis belladonna (sometimes known as the Belladonna lily) with yellow throats, pink carnations and unidentifiable daisy-like flowers in shades of pink, blue and yellow. These are set against a white ground decorated with green circles of irregular outline.

Mayfair (picture page 64)
Backstamp 8
Registration numbers for Canada 1951.
A rather widely spaced pattern having bouquets of chrysanthemums in cerise and pale rust and flat, blue anemone-like flowers, a few small cerise buds and trailing green leaves. The pattern is crisply depicted and the ground colour is an unusual pale greeny-yellow.

The name refers to an area in London.

May Festival (picture page 64)
Backstamp 9
At first sight this pattern could be mistaken for Peony. The flowers and leaves are identical, but the arrangement is slightly different. May Festival has a dark blue ground with the peony flowers and leaves in white, tinged here and there with pale to mid-blue. It can also be found with hand painting on the flowers, similar to June Festival.

Meaford 1938
This pattern is, so far, unknown in the United Kingdom. However, Meaford was mentioned in *The Pottery Gazette* in February 1938. 'Chintz patterns have always been a speciality in the 'Winton Ware', and we are able to announce that three new subjects – all of them hand-enamelled – are in course of preparation. These will be known respectively as Sandon, Meaford and Offley.'

It is, of course, possible that the advent of World War II prevented the issuing of these designs, as potteries were then confined to making only undecorated ware. However, some decorated ware was permitted to be made for export, so it might be that these patterns were made for export only.

Morning Glory (picture page 64)
Backstamp 9
A very bold pattern of the convolvulus flower can be seen twining its way across the sheet transfer printed pattern. Both flowers and leaves are in white with pale pink detailing. The ground colour is a deep wine, almost maroon colour.

Nantwich (picture page 64)
Backstamp 4
This features bunches of pink roses, some with yellow tones to the petals. The carnations are also in the same pink, again some having yellow toned petals. Large yellow daisy-like flowers are interspersed with small blue speedwells and the ground colour is black.

The name refers to a town near Crewe in Cheshire.

Offley 1938
This pattern is, so far, unknown in the United Kingdom. However, Offley was mentioned in *The Pottery Gazette* in February 1938. 'Chintz patterns have always been a speciality in the 'Winton Ware', and we are able to announce that three new subjects – all of them hand-enamelled – are in course of preparation. These will be known respectively as Sandon, Meaford and Offley.'

It is, of course, possible that the advent of World War II prevented the issuing of these designs, as potteries were then confined to making only undecorated ware. However, some decorated ware was permitted to be made for export, so it might be that these patterns were made for export only.

Old Cottage Chinz (picture page 65)
Backstamp 4
Cerise pink roses are enhanced by small flat blue flowers and green and yellow leaves. The other flower shown, accompanied by green leaves, closely resembles Allium, being of a globular shape formed by a myriad of tiny pink star shaped florets. The background is formed of tiny grey circular outlines on a white ground.

Orient (picture page 65)
Backstamp 8
Registration numbers for Canada 1953
A striking design which is more of a sheet transfer pattern rather than chintz. A white and green water lily floats on a black ground which is broken up by tiny yellow wavelets. The pattern is enhanced by sprays of pink blossom, possibly Prunus (Cherry) with green leaves. Green and yellow butterflies separate the flower clusters.

Oriental Fantasy (picture page 65)
Backstamp 9
A lively scene featuring oriental fishermen set against a black background. The men can be seen fishing and carrying their catch from moored boats to the harbour jetty. Other boats are dotted about and the scene also includes an island volcano surrounded by cherry trees. Blue waves enliven the picture, while grey and orange clouds seem to foretell a storm.

Scattered cherry blossoms and leaves can also be seen.

'Paisley' 1923 (picture page 65)
Backstamp 4
A busy all-over pattern, the paisley design can also be seen on items by manufacturers other than Royal Winton. Grimwades issued it in colourways of green and rust. The colours are vivid in the green colourway, with additional hues of turquoise, orange and yellow. The paisley swirls are accompanied by stylised flowers and leaves and are set against a white ground. The rust colourway uses shades varying from pale apricot through pale orange to deep rust. There is some minimal additional decoration in yellow. The ground colour is white.

There is also a blue colourway where colours of deep blue, tan and green are seen on a white ground, but this seems to appear mainly on ware by other manufacturers.

The design was illustrated in a Grimwades catalogue for 1923 when it was shown in an Elite shape jug.

Pebbles (picture page 66)
Backstamp 4
A sheet transfer printed pattern of simple style, Pebbles can be found in two colourways of green or a pale creamy yellow. The pattern consists of irregular pebble shapes, outlined in brown. The green alternates from a pale to a slightly darker hue. Pieces do not seem to bear the pattern name and this was identified by a Royal Winton employee.

Pekin (picture page 66)
Backstamp 9. Also found with; GRIMWADES ROYAL WINTON IVORY ENGLAND, and J-W. Co. STAFFORDSHIRE ENGLAND ROYAL WINTON (Backstamp 10). Some pieces are marked Hand Painted.
Registration numbers for Canada 1951.
This willow-pattern design was made with four different ground colours. The black colourway has subtle shadings of yellow, ochre and tan, with the highlights on the pagoda, bridge and boat picked out in a raspberry pink. Accompanying flowers and leaves are in shades of pink, white and yellow.

The pattern on the cream colourway is a little more well defined. Pink is used, as in the black version, but the trees and the foreground to the pagoda are picked out in delicate shades of green.

The blue colourway is again similar to the black Pekin but like the cream version, uses shades of green for the trees. The foreground of the pagoda is in shades of yellow and green.

The red colourway is quite striking and is possibly the first version to have been introduced, having the ROYAL WINTON IVORY backstamp. The pagoda roof, bridge and boat are in blue, the trees in green and lilac, while the foreground is green. There is additional hand enamelling which adds to the richness of the colouring.

Pelham 1935 (picture page 67)
Backstamp 4
This would appear to be the first in the range of needlepoint or sampler designs. Pelham shows a pretty design of pink, blue and yellow flowers set in an ornamental urn of pale blue having darker blue crossing lines. Small bouquets of flowers intersperse the urns and the background is composed of a graph paper design on a white ground. On close examination, Pelham can be seen to be a reduced version of the Sampler pattern.

The pattern was mentioned in *The Pottery Gazette* in April 1935 when reporting on the exhibition at Olympia. 'Good business was done with the new relief-modelled tablewares, and the 'Pelham' and 'Cranstone' chintz patterns were also very well received – more particularly so, perhaps, seeing that the Queen (Her Majesty, Queen Mary) purchased both of these patterns.'

Peony (picture page 67)
Backstamp 9
This is a very similar design to May Festival, but having the flowers differently arranged. The ground colour is black and the peony flowers are shown in shades of white and grey.

Queen Anne 1936 (picture page 67)
Backstamp 4, 8
Registration numbers for Canada (impressed) 1951; Australia Reg No 15541
This is another of the needlepoint or sampler patterns issued by Royal Winton, the first of which appears to be Pelham. The pattern consists of bouquets of flowers in pink, blue and yellow, accompanied by green leaves and executed in a cross-stitch style. The background is of grey graph paper on an ivory ground.

The Pottery Gazette previewing the British Industries Fair, commented in February 1936, 'Several fresh patterns in old English chintzes will also be on view, including a very pleasing 'sampler' design which has been named Queen Anne.'

Queen Mary, too, must have approved of the pattern, as an invoice from Grimwades, dated 15th July 1936, shows that Her Majesty ordered a Bowl No 1 in the Fife shape at a cost of 2/6d (12½ pence).

Quilt c1938 (picture page 67)
Backstamp 6
Gt Britain Rd No 824107 (c1938)
Registration numbers for Canada 10.1.38 (which appears to be a date); Australia 17469.
Quilt is a pattern which lives up to its name, and consists of various sections representing a patchwork of floral fabrics. They are arranged haphazardly and are in colours of pink, blue and black, with touches of yellow here and there. There is no ground colour to be seen.

Richmond (picture page 68)
Backstamp 4
The pattern on Richmond consists of an abundant design of bright yellow daffodils and white narcissi, with sprays of green leaves, bluebells and pink and blue hyacinths set against a pale green ground.

The name refers to towns in North Yorkshire and Greater London.

Rose du Barry – see 'Rose Violet'

'Rose Spray' (picture page 68)
Backstamp 9
A light and airy design of pink roses, smaller blue flowers and orange and yellow daffodils, all widely set against a white ground.

'Rose Sprig' (picture page 68)
Backstamp 4
This is a widely spaced pattern showing sprigs of flowers comprising a pink rose, a yellow starry flower, and several small violets, set against a vivid yellow ground.

In April 1940, *The Pottery Gazette* reported: 'Among other new styles there is a series of treatments with underglaze blown backgrounds relieved by scattered sprays of chintz. There are three different backgrounds – pink, green and yellow...The series has only been on the market a few weeks, but we learn that it has already secured good business.'

Close examination of 'Rose Sprig' would indicate that is possibly to this pattern that *The Pottery Gazette* was referring.

'Rose Violet' – now known to be Rose du Barry (picture page 68)
Backstamp 4
The pattern is one that has been used by several manufacturers other than Royal Winton. However, the piece illustrated is marked (See Backstamp 4). The design has a delicate appearance and consists of pale pink roses and violets accompanied by curving leaves in green and pale purple. The white ground enhances the pastel colours.

Royalty 1937 (picture page 69)
Backstamp 4, 8
This consists of a striking pattern of pale cerise anemones and vivid blue carnations accompanied by green and ochre leaves set against a pale yellow ground. Royalty is an alternative colourway to Majestic which features flowers in the same colour but on a black ground.

An invoice sent by Grimwades to Her Majesty Queen Mary on the 20th February 1937 shows that she ordered a Stafford twin tray, a covered muffin, a Chrysta powder box and a Burke powder box in the Royalty pattern. It is interesting to note that the twin tray cost 1/3d, the covered muffin cost 1/6d, while the powder boxes cost 10d each. In post-decimal money (new pence), that is respectively 6¼ pence, 7½ pence, 4 pence.

Rutland 1933/34 (picture page 69)
Registered number 768965.
Backstamp: words ROYAL WINTON (curved) with WINTON (below) transfer printed in green (See Backstamp 5). Also GRIMWADES ROYAL WINTON IVORY ENGLAND transfer printed in green.
A showy pattern of white, pink, ochre and blue daisies arranged in a bouquet, with smaller daisies in rust and blue, and accompanied by sprays of what appears to be yellow lilac. The ground colour is white.

Name refers to a now extinct English county.

Sampler (picture page 69)

Identical to Pelham, but printed as an enlarged version, Sampler is a pretty design of pink, blue and yellow flowers set in an ornamental urn of pale blue having darker blue crossing lines. Small bouquets of flowers intersperse the urns and the background is composed of a graph paper design on a white ground.

Sandon 1938

This pattern is, so far, unknown in the United Kingdom. However, Sandon was mentioned in *The Pottery Gazette* in February 1938. 'Chintz patterns have always been a speciality in the 'Winton Ware', and we are able to announce that three new subjects – all of them hand-enamelled – are in course of preparation. These will be known respectively as Sandon, Meaford and Offley.'

It is, of course, possible that the advent of World War II prevented the issuing of these designs, as potteries were then confined to making only undecorated ware. However, some decorated ware was permitted to be made for export, so it might be that these patterns were made for export only.

Name refers to towns in Staffordshire, Hertfordshire and Essex.

Shrewsbury (picture page 69)

Backstamp 8
Registration numbers for Canada 1952, Australia 29776.
Although the pattern consists of daisies, like Rutland, this has been given a far more serene treatment. The flowers are mainly of a soft pink, some petals tinged with yellow, with the occasional white daisy. The leaves are almost fern-like, the ground colour a creamy yellow/white.

Name refers to a town in Shropshire

Somerset (picture page 70)

Backstamp 4
The flower featured appears to closely resemble the lilac but, as the leaves are those of a delphinium, one can safely assume that it is the delphinium which is portrayed. Sprays of the blossom are closely packed together and are in colours of pink, blue and yellow, giving an effect totally unlike that of the Delphinium Chintz pattern, where the sprays are slightly more widely set. There is an accompaniment of green leaves, and the ground colour is a creamy yellow.

Name refers to a county in Southern England.

Spring (picture page 70)

Backstamp 4
This shows a large bouquet of flowers consisting of pink and yellow

roses, yellow daffodils and white narcissi. Pale lilac tulips and purple wisteria edge the bouquet which is interspersed with delicate green leaves. The same pattern features in both Hazel and Welbeck but against differently coloured backgrounds. The ground colour on Spring is white irregularly partitioned by small pebble shapes in grey.

Spring Glory (picture page 71)
Backstamp 9
A riotous display of yellow cowslips and pink, blue and white wild wood anemones forms this pattern. The green leaves are those of the cowslip and the black ground emphasises the delicate pastel colours.

Springtime 1932 (picture page71)
Backstamp MADE IN with ENGLAND curved below, transfer printed in green (See Backstamp 5).
A vigorous treatment of tulips features a bunch of the flowers in a bold cerise colour, shading to yellow at the base of each tulip. The tulips are accompanied by flat yellow and blue flowers and foliage set on a white ground.

The pattern was advertised in *The Pottery Gazette* in April 1932 when it was declared that the pattern was much in demand.

Stratford (picture page 71)
Backstamp 8
Registration numbers for Canada 1953.
Cerise and yellow tulips accompanied by green leaves decorate this attractive pattern. The flowers are complemented by small sprays of lilac plus their leaves, although, at first sight, the lilac can be mistaken for bunches of blackberries. The ground colour is in subtle shades of a delicate blue.

Name refers to an area in London.

Summertime 1930/31 (picture page 71)
Backstamp 4, 7, 8. Also seen marked with the words MADE IN ENGLAND in black transfer printed capitals. Some items were marked with the words Summertime COPYRIGHT Wright Tyndale & van Roden Inc ENGLAND transfer printed in blue in both script and capitals (Backstamp 7). This was presumably an American retailer.
Although not advertised until 1932, with Delphinium Chintz being advertised in *The Pottery Gazette* in 1931, Summertime was the second chintz pattern to be issued by Grimwades. The trade press was almost lyrical in its praise and a report in *The Pottery Gazette* in July 1932 reads, 'The trade will recall the old 'Marguerite Chintz', which, not many years ago, was a tremendous success. This has now been succeeded by a pattern which has been christened 'Summertime'. It is a sort of fantasia, compounded of roses, daisies, violets, harebells, and similar

summer-time flowers. This is said to have been taken up freely by many of the leading buyers, some of whom have not hesitated to pronounce it even an improvement upon the old 'Marguerite'; and to say that is to say a good deal.'

The pattern features all the flowers mentioned above, but the violets are rather indistinguishable.

It was also issued in a different colourway as Bedale, with the pattern featuring the roses in yellow and not pink.

Sunshine (picture page72)

Backstamp 4

A warmly coloured pattern evocative of its name, Sunshine has large anemone-like flowers in blue and in pink, with the petals shading to yellow, accompanied by smaller dark blue and white flowers and forget-me-nots. The green leaves and flowers have yellow shading merging with the minimal white ground.

Sweet Nancy (picture page72)

Backstamp 4

Bouquets of white narcissi and what appear to be wallflowers are the theme of this design. Background flowers resembling lilacs are accompanied by tiny yellow flowers set against a cream ground

Sweet Pea 1936 (picture page 72)

Backstamp 4
Registration numbers for Australia 15538

Vivid blossoms of the sweet pea in colours of pink, deep blue, deep yellow and white are arranged against a background of leaves and coiling tendrils. The ground colour varies from a pale cream to a deep yellow/ochre.

An invoice from Grimwades to H.M. Queen Mary, dated the 15th July 1936, shows that Her Majesty ordered tea pot number 12, Athena shape, in this pattern, priced at 2/- (10 pence) and a salad bowl and servers No 2 and No 2A in King shape at a cost of 3/6d (17½ pence).

Tartans c1937 (picture page 73)

Backstamp 6
Gt Britain Rd No 824091 c1937.
Registration numbers for Canada 23.12.37 (which appears to be a date); Australia 17468.

Various overlapping scraps of plaids in bright colours form the basis of this pattern. Combined colours of blue, green, scarlet, orange and beige are crossed and bisected with lines of yellow, black, blue, green and white, giving an attractive but jumbled effect.

Victorian (picture page 73)
Backstamp 4
Another needlepoint or sampler pattern, Victorian is an alternative colourway to Queen Anne. The pattern consists of bouquets of flowers in pink, blue and yellow, accompanied by green leaves and executed in a cross-stitch effect. The graph paper effect is of white squares on a black ground.

Her Majesty Queen Mary ordered a Bowl No 3 in the Victorian pattern at a cost of 2/6d (12½ pence) and the invoice is dated the 15th July 1936.

Victorian Rose (picture page 73)
Backstamp 4, 8
Registration numbers for Canada 1953
The pattern shows dark pink roses arranged in a bouquet with smaller flat blue flowers interspersed. An occasional half-opened yellow rosebud is also seen. The flowers are fairly widely spaced against the white ground.

'Violets' (picture page 74)
Backstamp 4
An extremely pretty design of purple violets and vivid yellow primroses, delicately enhanced by green and pale purple leaves. The ground colour is ivory.

Welbeck (picture page 74)
Backstamp 4
This shows a large bouquet of flowers consisting of pink and yellow roses, yellow daffodils and white narcissi. Pale lilac tulips and purple wisteria, rather indistinctly coloured, edge the bouquet which is interspersed with delicate green leaves.

The same pattern features in both Hazel and Spring but against differently coloured backgrounds. The ground colour of Welbeck is yellow, irregularly partitioned by small pebble shapes in ochre.

'White Roses' (picture page 75)
Pattern number possibly 1575
Backstamp 8
Roses, shaded in white and grey, are seen scattered across a lemon yellow ground. Small grey and even smaller black leaves highlight the ground colour.

Wild Flowers (picture page 75)

Backstamp 4, 5

Wild flowers are scattered across what seems to be a background of yellow mimosa balls. The white flowers are unidentifiable but the blue spray is probably Wood Vetch, while the flat pink flower closely resembles the Dianthus armeria known as Deptford pink.

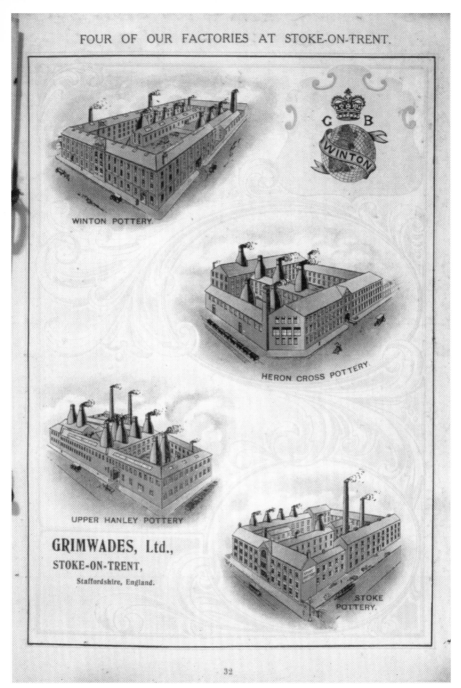

FOUR OF OUR FACTORIES AT STOKE-ON-TRENT.

WINTON POTTERY.

HERON CROSS POTTERY.

UPPER HANLEY POTTERY

GRIMWADES, Ltd.,
STOKE-ON-TRENT,
Staffordshire, England.

STOKE POTTERY.

32

An artist's impression of the Winton, Heron Cross, Upper Hanley and Stoke Potteries as shown in a Grimwades catalogue for 1913. (Courtesy Peter Greenhalf)

Anemone: A large bread and butter plate with dark blue ground and an Art Deco diamond-shaped dish on a mid-blue ground.

Balmoral: An **Ascot** shape bread and butter plate, a small **Countess** teapot, and a shaped, rectangular sweet dish.

Bedale: An un-footed fruit bowl in the **Stafford** shape.

Beeston: An Art Deco trio of cup, saucer and plate in the **Hastings** shape.

Birds and Tulips: A wide, angular cup and saucer in the Art Deco style, edged with gilding.

Blue Anemone (Chintz): An Art Deco teapot in the **Norman** shape.

Blue Jade: A small **Countess** milk jug.

Blue Tulip: A cream jug in the **Ascot** shape and a coffee can and saucer.

Cheadle: A flower vase in Cintra shape, a large **Countess** teapot, a footed bon-bon dish (up-ended), a preserve pot with matching lid and stand in the **Ascot** shape and a cup and saucer. (Courtesy of Beverley)

Chelsea: A hot water jug and a large bread and butter plate in the **Ascot** shape. (Courtesy of Beverley)

Clevedon: A fluted oval dish, a small basket in the **Hampton** shape and a footed bon bon dish. *(Courtesy of Beverley)*

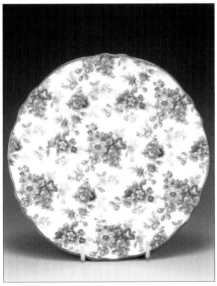

Clyde: An **Ascot** bread and butter plate, an oblong sweet dish in the **Athena** shape and a tennis set.

Cotswold: A round tea plate.

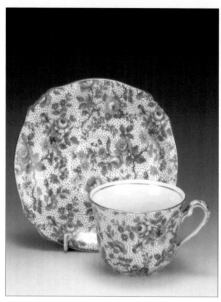

Cranstone: A cup and saucer.

Crocus (Black): A large round bread and butter plate, a small cream jug in the Globe shape and a small oval dish.

Crocus (White): A small oblong sandwich plate in the Ascot shape.

Cromer: A covered 2-handled sugar bowl in the Countess shape and an angular Hastings shape cup & saucer. (Courtesy of Beverley)

Delphinium Chintz: An up-ended footed comport. *(Courtesy of Beverley)*

Dorset: A large round plate and a coffee pot.

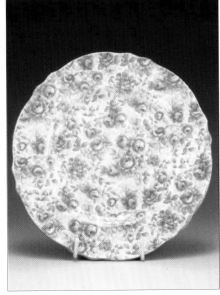

Eleanor: A 2-handled lamp base.

English Rose: A tea plate. *(Courtesy of Beverley)*

Estelle: A tea plate

Esther: An oblong sandwich tray with shaped ends and an **Ascot** cream jug.

Evesham: A large round teapot, a tennis set and a handled beaker or mug. *(Courtesy of Beverley)*

Exotic Bird: A large jug in the **Dutch** shape and a **Winton** shape cream jug.

Fernese: An oblong sweet dish in the Art Deco style.

Fireglow (Black): A small square sweet dish, a large oval dish and a **Countess** jug.

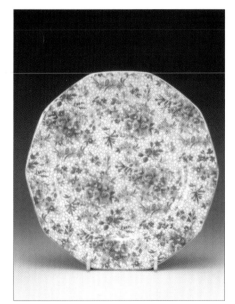

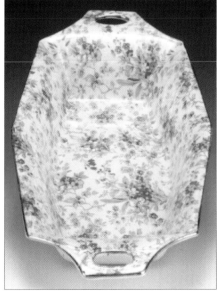

Fireglow (White): A ten-sided cheese plate in the **Octron** shape.

Floral Feast: A long, deep dished roll tray with open work handles in the **Fife** shape.

Florence: A cheese dish in the **Dane** *shape with a plain handle, a footed comport and a mint boat and stand in the* **Era** *shape. (Courtesy of Beverley)*

Gold Leaves: Cream ground tennis set of a size which is larger than usual.

Hazel: A jug/flower vase in the **Remus** *shape, a jardiniere, an* **Athena** *teapot and a smaller* **Ascot** *teapot. (Courtesy of Beverley)*

GRIMWADES LTD., WINTON POTTERY. STOKE-ON-TRENT.

Florette: Page from the Grimwades catalogue for 1930. (Courtesy Peter Greenhalf)

Jacobina: A square sweet dish with shaped 'handles' in the green colourway, an oval 3-sectioned hors d'oeuvre dish in white and a small butter dish in the Trefoil shape in the blue colourway

Japan: An **Ascot** shape cream jug.

Joyce-Lynn: A large breakfast trio comprising a cup, saucer and plate.

Julia: A 2-handled sweet dish, a 3-piece cruet with chromed tops, a handled beaker or mug, a tennis set and a covered butter dish. *(Courtesy of Beverley)*

June Festival: A large round plate; a hand painted mint boat stand.

June Roses: An **Ascot** cake plate on a chromed stand.

Kew: A mint boat stand in blue and a tea plate.

Kinver: A large jug in the **Dutch** shape and a small hexagonal sugar in the **Hector** shape.

Majestic: A small deep sweetmeat dish with shaped ends and a **Globe** sugar bowl.

Marion: A musical box; a tennis set; one of a pair of salad servers.

Marguerite: Left: A Mecca foot warmer, first introduced in 1913. and (right) A muffin dish with blue edging and a strawberry shaped knob in white outlined in blue, a cream jug of **Vera** shape and an Atlas China cup and saucer edged with gilding and transfer printed with the pattern on both the inside and the outside of the cup.

Marguerite: A page from the 1928 Grimwades catalogue. (Courtesy Peter Greenhalf)

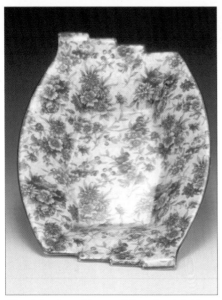

Mayfair: An oblong dish with Art Deco styled stepped 'handles'. *(Courtesy of Beverley)*

May Festival: A round tea plate; a covered butter dish.

Morning Glory: A large bread and butter plate in the **Ascot** shape.

Nantwich: An Ascot bread and butter plate, a coffee pot, an open sugar bowl, a cream jug and a coffee cup and saucer. *(Courtesy of Beverley)*

Old Cottage Chintz: A round tea plate and a double egg cup, used for both duck and hen's eggs.

Old Cottage Chintz: A round tea plate and a double egg cup, used for both duck and hen's eggs.

Oriental Fantasy: A sandwich tray in the **Ascot** shape.

Paisley: A coffee pot in the **Greek** shape, and a green colourway sandwich tray in the **Ascot** shape.

Paisley: The coffee pot in the blue colourway shows an identical pattern, but was not made by Royal Winton.

Pebbles: A footed bon-bon dish.

Pekin: A small, red hand painted plate, a blue pin tray (Backstamp 10), a black **Countess** teapot and a cream coffee cup and saucer.

Pelham: A small sweet dish in the **Ascot** shape.

Peony: An up-ended **Globe** sugar bowl and a small **Globe** jug.

Queen Anne: A tea plate in the **Ascot** shape and a candy box (impressed CANDY BOX).

Quilt: A small oval dish; a sugar sifter.

Richmond: Cheese dish in the **Dane** shape with an ornate handle. The cheese dish was available in 3 sizes.

Rose Spray: Cheese dish in the **Dane** shape, available in 3 sizes. The example shown has a plain handle.

Rose Sprig: A canoe-shaped long dish.

Rose Violet (Rose du Barry): A three-piece cruet on a trefoil-shaped stand.

Royalty: A chamberstick and a jam or preserve pot with matching lid and base in the **Ascot** shape.

Rutland: An angular Art Deco cup and saucer in the **Hastings** shape.

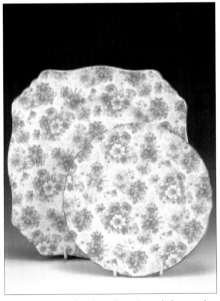

Sampler: A beaker.

Shrewsbury: An **Ascot** cake plate and a round tea plate.

Somerset: A large cake plate in the **Orleans** *shape, a salad bowl with a silver plated rim in the* **Rheims** *shape and a bedside set comprising a* **Countess** *teapot, a cup, a cream jug, an open sugar bowl and a toast rack. (Courtesy of Beverley)*

Spring: An **Ascot** *cream jug and sugar bowl, a cream jug in the* **Grecian** *shape (shown standing on a wooden block) and an* **Ascot** *teapot.*

Spring Glory: Tray from a bedside set.

Springtime: Preserve or honey pot with silver plated lid.

Stratford: A small rimmed soup or dessert dish and a 2 piece cruet set on a matching base.

Summertime: A wall clock and a small **Countess** teapot.

Sunshine: A footed bon bon dish; a stacking set of teapot, cream and sugar in the **Delamere** shape. *(Courtesy of Beverley)*

Sweet Nancy: Two-handled oval sweetmeat dish.

Sweet Pea: A bedside set comprising a **Countess** teapot, a cup, a cream jug, an open sugar bowl and a toast rack, a biscuit barrel, an **Athena** shape teapot, a 3-bar toast rack and a pair of salad servers. *(Courtesy of Beverley)*

Tartans: An **Ascot** *tea plate and a 3-bar toast rack.*

Victorian: Small tea plate in the **Ascot** shape.

Victorian Rose: An **Ascot** *sandwich plate and a 3-bar toast rack.*

Violets: An oval sweetmeat dish with curving Art Deco style 'handles'.

Welbeck: An Art Deco shaped fruit bowl; a **King** *shape cup and saucer.*

White Roses: *A biscuit barrel in the* **Rheims** *shape.*

Wild Flowers: *An egg cup stand (minus the egg cups) and a small butter pat dish in the* **Trefoil** *shape.*

Sheet of lithograph in the Joyce-Lynn pattern, and two pieces of ware which show the additional brightness of colour achieved after firing. (Courtesy Peter Greenhalf)

Pattern No. 4461 (c1922) and Pattern No. 4325 (c1920).

Jacobean patterned Chamber pot, Pattern No. 3000 (c1913) plus vase c1917-18 and triple dish Pattern No. 4252 (c1917/18).

STRUMA
4444
31/- .. 6 piece Set.

STRUMA
4426
42/- .. 6 piece Set.

STRUMA
4427
42/- .. 6 piece Set.

WEIMAR
4461
29/- .. 6 piece Set.

STRUMA
4413
42/- .. 6 piece Set.

STRUMA
4408
42/- .. 6 piece Set.

KENSINGTON
4325
42/- .. 6 piece Set

DELPHIC
4435
37/- .. 6 piece Set.

STRUMA
4464
35/- .. 6 piece Set.

London Showrooms: 13, ST. ANDREW STREET, E.C.

Telephone: Holborn 1279.

Toilet sets in all-over floral patterns as shown in a Grimwades catalogue for 1922. (Courtesy Peter Greenhalf)

Grimwades *"Spode"* Chintz illustrated in a 1913 catalogue. (Courtesy Peter Greenhalf)

78

"FERNESE" DIAPER WARE
8786 (Registered).

SANDWICH SET.
5/-
Lots of 1 dozen sets 4/9

PRICES OF "FERNESE" DIAPER (8786).

JUG "DUTCH" Large — 5/- per set of 3.   Smaller Set — 4/6 per set.
  " "GRAFTON" — — 4/6 " "
  " Hot Water "GRAFTON" E.P.N.S. Pint size, 2/6; 1¼ pint, 2/9
CHEESE "REX" Medium size, 3/3   Small, 2/9
TEAPOT "ELITE" Large, 2/10   Medium, 2/8   Small, 2/6
STANDS — 13/- doz.
21-PIECE TEA SETS "STAFFORD" Shape, 9/6
SANDWICH SET, 5/-   TEAPOT SET, 6/6
Also supplied in this pattern :—PATENT CUBE TEAPOT (in 4 sizes) 24's, 3/9 ; 30's, 3/6 ; 36's, 3/3 ; 42's, 3/-
    WINDSOR BOWL, 2/4 each.   TRIPLE TRAY, 4/9, WATERCRESS, 4/6, HONEY POT, 2/3

GRIMWADES LTD., WINTON POTTERY, STOKE-ON-TRENT.

Ferenese Diaper ware as shown in the Grimwades catalogue for 1925. (Courtesy Peter Greenhalf)

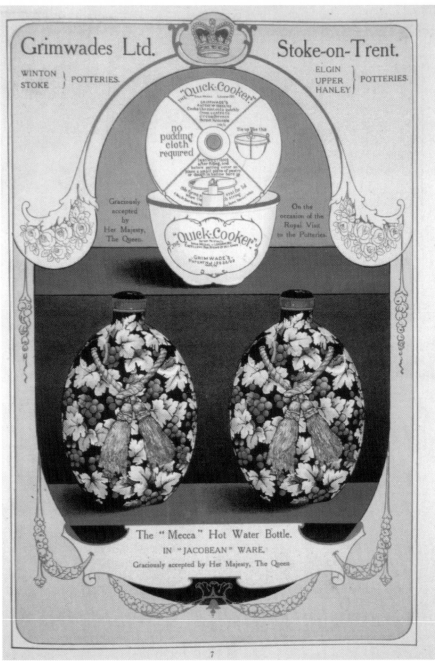

A page from the 1913 catalogue showing Grimwades' famous **Quick-Cooker** and the **Mecca Footwarmer**. (Courtesy Peter Greenhalf)

Shapes

The name of the shape was often impressed in the base of the piece and this has proved helpful to collectors, but as post 1930 catalogues for Royal Winton wares seem to be non-existent, it has not been possible to identify all the shapes. Often, the shape name applied only to single items in the following list, although it is almost certain that other items were also made in the same shape. However, for accuracy, only known items are identified.

Sources and references are given wherever possible. If a shape is illustrated in the book, then an example of the pattern in that shape will be given.

If no illustration for a shape exists, then as full a description as possible will be given. This is not always practical, however, as some shapes are mentioned in catalogues and The Pottery Gazette but without illustration.

Shape Names	Product	Pattern illustrated
Ajax	Tea ware	No illustration

This shape was illustrated in a 1930s Grimwades catalogue, and was shown as a fluted 8 or 10-sided cup and 10-sided saucer in both a 'tall' shape (with straight-sided body and a high pointed handle) and a 'low' shape which had straight-sided body tapering sharply to the foot and having an uplifted, squared- off handle, rather like Hastings. The teapot appears to be octagonal, having a squared-off handle and an open rectangular handle to the teapot lid.

Shape Names	Product	Pattern illustrated
Ascot	Cream jug	Esther, "Blue Tulip"
(Shape No. 970)	Plate: large	Balmoral
	: sandwich	Victorian Rose
	: tea	Queen Anne
	Preserve pot	Cheadle, Royalty
	Sugar bowl	Pekin, Spring
	Sweet dish	Pelham
	Teapot	Hazel

The tea ware was advertised with a full page illustration in *The Pottery Gazette* in November 1932. The pattern shown was Cherry Blossom, a non-chintz design.

Note: Ascot can easily be confused with Athena. For an example, compare the base of the teapots in the Hazel illustration. The base of the Ascot teapot is flat and straight while the base of the Athena teapot is indented, giving the impression of small feet.

Athena	Bowl, 6 sizes	No illustration
	Sweet dish	Clyde
	Teapot	Sweet Pea, Hazel

The bowl was mentioned in a Grimwades catalogue in 1930. No description was given.

The tea ware was advertised with a full page illustration in *The Pottery Gazette* in September 1934.

Note: Athena can easily be confused with Ascot. For an example, compare the base of the teapots in the Hazel illustration. The base of the Athena teapot is indented, giving the impression of small feet, while the base of the Ascot teapot is flat and straight.

| Burke | Powder Box | No illustration |

Queen Mary purchased a powder box in this shape in the Royalty pattern in February 1937. The Grimwades catalogue for 1923 shows this to be of round, squat, bulbous appearance, widening towards the base. The overlapping lid had no finial or handle with which to lift it.

| Cambridge | Jug, squarish | No illustration |

| Candy Box | Rectangular box | Queen Anne |

The words CANDY BOX are impressed on the base of this piece. A catalogue for 1930 shows this listed as an "Oblong" Box.

| Chelsea | Preserve pot | No illustration |

The preserve pot is of globular form and has a round lid with a squarish knob. The separate stand is also round.

| Chrysta | Powder Box | No illustration |

A Grimwades invoice shows that Queen Mary purchased a powder box in this shape in the Royalty pattern in February 1937. No description was given.

| Cintra | Flower vase | Cheadle |

Countess	Covered sugar bowl	Cromer
	Jug, various sizes	Fireglow (Black)
	Teapot	Pekin

Note: The shape of the jug can easily be confused with that of Globe. However, careful comparison will show that the pouring lip of Countess is narrower and slightly more upward pointing than that of Globe.

| Crown | Bowl in sizes 6½", 8" and 9" | Marguerite catalogue illustration |

| Dane | Biscuit barrel with wicker handle | No illustration |

| | Bowl 5″ | Florette catalogue illustration |
| | Cheese dish | "Rose Spray" and Richmond |

A cheese dish in the Dane shape used was first produced in 1913. The open rectangular handle was ornately moulded but in the 1930s and onwards, a plain, simple handle was also available. Richmond has an ornate handle; "Rose Spray" is plain.

A Grimwades catalogue for 1922 shows the biscuit barrel to be of rounded form tapering to a footed base. The top is indented at the handles, flaring out to the rim. There is a round knob on the lid.

| **Delamere** | Stacking set of teapot, cream and sugar | Sunshine |

| **Delius** | Jug/ewer | No illustration |

A tall handled jug or ewer having a bulbous base and going in at the 'waist' before widening briefly and narrowing again. The jug then flares widely at the top.

| **Duchess** | Teapot | No illustration |

A teapot in the Duchess shape was purchased by Queen Mary in February 1937. No pattern name was shown on the Grimwades invoice, only the pattern number 3030.

Duchess dinner ware was illustrated in a Grimwades catalogue for 1925/28. However, no illustration was shown for tea ware.

| **Dutch** | Jug, various sizes | Kinver |

This shape was first mentioned in a catalogue dated 1923.

| **Duval** | Jug, 3 sizes | Florette and Marguerite catalogue illustrations |

Elite	Jug stand	Marguerite catalogue illustration
	Teapot	Florette and Marguerite catalogue illustrations
	(3 sizes)	

This shape was first illustrated in a Grimwades catalogue dated 1923 when it featured an Elite cream jug in the Paisley pattern. The shape is round and globular - a rounder and flatter version of the Globe jug. The teapot is also round and globular, with a strawberry finial to the lid.

Era	Mint boat/stand	Florence

Etona Vase No illustration
Of tubular form, the vase is wider at the base than the top. It curves gently inward to about half its height, then curves outward slightly.

Fife	Bowl	No illustration
	Roll tray	Florette catalogue illustration
	Sandwich tray	Floral Feast

A Fife Bowl No. 1 in the Queen Anne pattern was purchased by Queen Mary on the 15th July 1937. The bowls were made in various sizes.
Fife supper sets, consisting of a slightly dished tray with six small tea plates, were illustrated in a Grimwades catalogue for 1930.

Gem Rose bowl No illustration
A round globular bowl with a short stem and wide foot. It was fitted with a brass grid-like top to hold the roses in place.

Globe	Jug, 4 sizes	Crocus, Peony
	Sugar bowl	Majestic, Peony
	Teapot, 3 sizes	No illustration
	Teapot stand	No illustration

The teapot first went into production in 1896 and is known to have been made, still in the same shape, until at least 1925/28. The teapot is round and globular with a slight foot rim. The lid sits snugly inside the collar of the pot and has a mushroom shaped knob or finial. It is not known whether or not it was made in chintz patterns.
Note: The shape of the jug can easily be confused with that of Countess. Careful examination will show that the pouring lip of Globe is wider and more shallow than that of Countess.

Gordon Candy dish No illustration
No description is available, other than the lid or cover has a pointed top.

Grecian Cream jug Spring

Greek	Coffee pot 1¼ pint	"Paisley"
	Jug stand	No illustration

The Greek shape, introduced in 1918 was used on various items of tableware, including salad bowls, biscuit jars, honey pots (with fast stands) and lids etc. The coffee pot shape of this period more resembled a hot water jug, its spout more of a large pouring lip; it was later modified to the shape shown in "Paisley".

Grosvenor	Posy bowl	No illustration

A hexagonal globular bowl, the top being of a slightly larger diameter than the base.

Hampton	Basket	Clevedon

First shown in a Grimwades catalogue dated 1930.

Hastings	Cup and saucer	Beeston, Rutland
Hector	Sugar bowl	Kinver
Hurstmere	Sugar bowl, 31/4"	Marguerite catalogue illustration
Imperial	Coffee cup/saucer	Florette catalogue illustration
Jacobean	Tea ware	No illustration

A cream and sugar set (private collection) show the jug has a sharply angular handle, similar to Hastings. The piece narrows towards the base in three 'steps'.

King	Cup and saucer	Cheadle, Welbeck
	Salad bowl	No illustration

A salad bowl and servers No 2 and No 2A, in the Sweet Pea pattern, was sold to Queen Mary on the 15th July 1936.

Lotus	Honey jar with lid	Marguerite catalogue
	(no stand)	illustration

Lotus tea ware is illustrated in a 1930 catalogue. The cup is slightly flared with a sharp indentation to the base. The handle is upwardly pointed. A sweet dish described as Lotus shape is shown in the Marguerite catalogue illustration. This was a mis-print, corrected in the price list in the same catalogue. The correct name for the shape is Octron.

Mecca	Foot warmer	Marguerite
Muffin	Covered muffin	Marguerite
Musical Box	Rectangular box	Marion
Nita	Wall pocket	No illustration

This is of an in-curving, elongated tulip shape, narrowing at the base to a small knob. There are two scrolling 'handles' halfway down each side of the pocket. The open top is formed by three arcs, the centre curve being wider than the two flanking arcs. Could possibly be described as a fleur-de-lys shape.

Norman	Teapot	"Blue Anemone" (Chintz)

Tea ware in this shape was illustrated in the Buyers' Notes section of The Pottery Gazette in July 1932, with a full page advertisement for Beverley patterned dinner ware (a non-chintz pattern) shown in the same publication in December 1932.

Octavius	Bowl (8-sided)	Florette catalogue illustration
	Bon bon or chocolate comport	No illustration

The comport was mentioned in a 1930s catalogue price list, when it was sold for 19/6 (97 1/2 pence) per dozen.

Octron	Plate	Fireglow (White)
	Sweet dish (8-sided)	Florette catalogue illustration

The plate has ten sides despite the shape name which would indicate an 8-sided shape, but reference to a Grimwade catalogue for 1930 confirms this rather odd anomaly. There appears to be no dictionary definition of the word Octron.

The same sweet dish is shown in the Marguerite catalogue illustration under the name of Lotus. This was a misprint and was corrected in the price list in the same catalogue.

Orleans	Plate, large	Somerset

The catalogue for 1925/28 shows that a rectangular Orleans sandwich plate, together with six square tea plates, was sold as a sandwich or supper set.

Remus	Large vase/jug	Hazel

Rex	Triple tray	Illustration of Pattern Number 4252
	Cheese dish	Marguerite catalogue
	3 sizes: No. 1, 2 and 2a	illustration

The Rex cheese dish was introduced in 1913 when it had a slightly fluted body. Later cheese dishes from the 1930s period kept the same general shape but had a more squared-off body.

Rheims	Salad bowl with chromed rim	Somerset
	Biscuit barrel	White Rose

The biscuit barrel is also shown in the Marguerite catalogue illustration (at the bottom left hand corner of the picture) with a slightly different knob to the lid.

Rosa   Wall pocket   No illustration
A double wall pocket of elongated triangular shape ending in a curved point. The pockets appear to overlap each other in a stepped manner and are enhanced by the addition of 3 semicircular 'ears' on one side of the pocket.

Rowsley   Basket   No illustration
The handled basket has a wavy rim and flares from the footed base in a high sided gondola shape.

Ryde   Ashtray   No illustration
A rectangular ashtray of Art Deco form with an irregular, stepped interior.

Shell   Butter/jam dish   No illustration
This small dish is shaped and fluted rather like a cockle shell.

Stafford	Fruit bowl	Marguerite catalogue illustration
	Long tray	Marguerite catalogue illustration
	Watercress dish and stand	No illustration

A Stafford tea cup, illustrated in a Grimwades catalogue for 1930, shows a wide cup tapering to the base with a sharp inward indentation to the foot. The squarish handle is slightly upward pointing.

The water cress dish and stand was first mentioned in a price list for 1925/28 and then cost 3/6d (17½ pence). Dinner ware also appeared in the same catalogue.

Stella	Fruit set with a 9" bowl	Marguerite catalogue illustration

Tennis Set	Cup with matching saucer/plate	Mayfair, "Gold Leaves"

Queen Mary purchased 6 tennis sets in pattern 4808 at a cost of 1/- (5 pence) each in February 1939. The tennis set in the "Gold Leaves" pattern is larger than usual.

| Troy | Fruit bowl | Marguerite catalogue |
| | square 9" | illustration (lower half of the page) |

Tea ware in the Troy shape was also made c1925/28 for Atlas China, a factory which was part of the Grimwades group.

| Trefoil | Butter pat dish | Wild Flowers |

| Tudor | Vase | No illustration |

A vase of tubular tapering form, narrowing from the top to a wide base.

| Vera | Cream jug | Marguerite |

| Winton | Cream jug 2oz, 4oz, 8oz, 10oz. | "Exotic Bird" and Marguerite catalogue illustration |

The Winton shape first went into production in 1922.

Price Guide

The prices given below are, of necessity, for guidance only. Royal Winton chintz ware is extremely collectable, and prices can, and do, fluctuate. Several factors govern this fluctuation. For instance, a plate in a certain pattern might cost three or four times the price of a plate in another, different pattern as some patterns are far more collectable than others. However, the desirability of these patterns can vary depending on which part of the country - or even in which country - one might be buying.

Shapes contribute to the price, too. For example, a cream jug in the Grecian shape will command a far higher price than a cream jug of an identical pattern in the more common Globe shape.

The rarity of the item also has to be considered. Wall clocks and musical boxes are not commonly found, while wall pockets are sought after, especially those of an angular Art Deco shape. Bedside sets (or breakfast sets, as they are also known) are collectors' items, too. There is also quite a demand for small, unusual pieces, such as a stand with egg cups and tiny matching salt and pepper pots.

The price guide refers to items in perfect condition, having no chips, cracks, or restoration. The transfer printing should be of the highest quality, with no unsightly over-lapping or creases.

Collectors should take the above facts into consideration when debating whether or not to go ahead with a purchase. They will also have to bear in mind that, as the chintz market fluctuates, prices can, and will, vary, depending on what is fashionable and desirable at the time.

The price guide below has been classified as follows:

A: refers to items of common and/or readily available patterns in routine shapes.

B: covers pieces which are less readily seen and/or are of more interesting shapes

C: takes into account the rarity and/or collectability of the pattern, or shapes that are different, unusual, or seldom seen. Although an upper limit has been given, there is no real ceiling for items that are extra special.

Note: Prices in America, Canada and Australia will often be much higher than the estimates quoted below.

Group A

Baskets:	
small	£30-£40/$50-$70
medium	£50-£70/$85-$120
large	£80-£100/$135-$170
Beakers and mugs	£20-£30/$35-$50
Bedside sets	£70-£100/$120-$170
Biscuit barrels	£40-£80/$70-$135
Candy boxes	£30-£60/$50-$100
Canoes	£20-£40/$35-$70
Cheese dishes	£40-£60/$70-$100
Coffee pots	£30-£60/$50-$100
Cruets:	
2-piece + stand	£25-£35/$40-$60
3-piece + stand	£30-£40/$50-$100
Cups and saucers:	
breakfast	£25-£35/$40-$60
coffee	£15-£25/$25-$40
tea	£25-£35/$40-$60
trios	£30-£40/$50-$70
Delamere stacking sets	£60-£100/$100-$170
Egg cups	£10-£15/$15-$25
Footed bon-bon dishes	£25-£40/$40-$70
Footed comports	£40-£60/$70-$100
Fruit bowls	£30-£60/$50-$100
Fruit dishes	£15-£25/$25-$40
Jam/Honey pots	£20-£30/$35-$50
Jugs, cream	£20-£30/$35-$50
Jugs, milk:	
small	£25-£40/$40-$70
medium	£30-£45/$50-$75
large	£50-£65/$85-$110
Mecca Foot Warmers	£150-£250/£255-$400

Group B	Group C
£40-£80/$70-$135	£80-£120/$135-$205
£70-£100/$120-$170	£100-£200/$170-$340
£100-£160/$170-$275	£160-£250/$275-$425
£30-£60/$50-$100	£60-£90/$100-$155
£150-£250/$255-$425	£250-£450/$425-$765
£80-£120/$135-$205	£120-£250/$205-$425
£60-£100/$100-$170	£100-£150/$170-$255
£40-£80/$70-$135	£80-£150/$135-$255
£60-£80/$100-$135	£80-£150/$135-$255
£60-£90/$100-$155	£90-£200/$155-$340
£35-£70/$60-$120	£70-£100/$120-$170
£40-£80/$70-$135	£80-£120/$135-$205
£35-£50/$60-$85	£50-£70/$85-$120
£25-£40/$40-$70	£40-£65/$70-$110
£35-£55/$60-$95	£55-£75/$95-$135
£40-£60/$70-$100	£60-£90/$100-$155
£100-£200/$170-$340	£200-£300/$340-$510
£15-£25/$25-$40	£25-£50/$40-$85
£40-£70/$70-$120	£70-£100/$120-$170
£60-£90/$100-$155	£90-£150/$155-$255
£60-£90/$100-$155	£90-£150/$155-$255
£25-£40/$40-$70	£40-£70/$70-$120
£30-£60/$50-$100	£60-£90/$100-$155
£30-£60/$50-$100	£60-£90/$100-$155
£40-£70/$70-$120	£70-£100/$120-$170
£45-£80/$75-$135	£80-£120/$135-$205
£65-£100/$110-$170	£100-£200/$170-$340
£250-£350/$425-$595	£350-£600/$425-$1020

Mint boats + stands	£20-£35/$35-$60
Muffin dishes	£40-£60/$70-$100
Musical boxes	£60-£80/$100-$135
Plates:	
small	£10-£15/$15-$25
medium	£15-£20/$25-$30
large	£25-£35/$40-$60
Salad bowls	£40-£60/$70-$100
Salad servers (pairs)	£30-£50/$50-$85
Sandwich trays:	
small	£15-£25/$25-$40
medium	£20-£35/$35-$60
large	£30-£45/$50-$80
Sugar bowls:	
open	£15-£20/$25-$35
covered	£25-£40/$40-$70
Sugar sifters	£25-£40/$40-$70
Teapots:	
small	£25-£40/$40-$70
medium	£50-£80/$85-$135
large	£60-£80/$100-$135
Tennis sets	£25-£40/$40-$70
Toast racks:	
3-bar	£20-£40/$35-$70
5-bar	£30-£50/$50-$85
Wall clocks	£40-£60/$70-$100
Wall pockets	£50-£80/$85-$135
Vases:	
small	£15-£25/$25-$40
medium	£30-£50/$50-$85
large	£50-£80/$65-$135

£35-£60/$60-$100
£60-£90/$100-$155
£80-£120/$135-$205

£60-£90/$100-$155
£90-£150/$155-$255
£120-£250/$205-$425

£15-£20/$25-$35
£20-£30/$35-$50
£35-£50/$60-$85
£60-£85/$100-$145
£50-£90/$85-$155

£20-£30/$35-$50
£30-£40/$50-$70
£50-£75/$85-$130
£85-£120/$145-$205
£90-£150/$155-$255

£25-£50/$40-$85
£35-£60/$60-$100
£45-£70/$75-$120

£50-£80/$85-$135
£60-£90/$100-$105
£70-£120/$120-$205

£20-£35/$35-$60
£40-£65/$70-$110
£40-£70/$70-$120

£35-£50/$60-$85
£65-£90/$110-$155
£70-£100/$120-$170

£40-£80/$70-$135
£80-£150/$135-$255
£80-£180/$135-$305
£40-£65/$70-$110

£80-£120/$135-$205
£150-£280/$255-$475
£180-£350/$305-$580
£65-£80/$110-$135

£40-£60/$70-$100
£50-£70/$85-$120
£60-£90/$100-$155
£80-£170/$135-$290

£60-£90/$100-$155
£70-£100/$120-$170
£90-£120/$125-$205
£170-£280/$290-$475

£25-£50/$40-$85
£50-£100/$85-$170
£80-£150/$135-$255

£50-£100/$85-$170
£100-£200/$170-$340
£150-£300/$255-$510

Backstamps

The manufacturer's trademark stamped on the base of ware is a useful guide to dating. These marks were changed periodically and new ones introduced. However, some overlapping of dates occurs and precise dating cannot be guaranteed.

It was thought that the prefix Royal was added to the Winton trade name in the 1930s. However, research has shown that Royal Winton ware was being made in 1896 (See chapter on Products). The name was used again in 1917/18 (See Backstamp 2). It then disappeared, being revived in about 1929, when Grimwades introduced their new Royal Winton Ivory. However, examples of Marguerite chintz, made in 1928, show the Royal Winton backstamp used in the familiar Art Deco style. It is interesting to note that the Home Office have no record of the company contacting them regarding the prefix.

In 1945, as a result of World War II, potteries were divided into six groups and obliged to mark their wares with a letter or letters of the alphabet, according to which group they belonged. They were also restricted to making tea and dinner ware, cooking ware including pie dishes, washstand sets, chamber pots, hot water bottles and stoppers and rolling pins.

The 1948 Year Book, issued by The Pottery Gazette shows that Grimwades were designated category 'A'. The letter had to be stamped indelibly under the glaze and the ruling was in force for some years after the war. For an example, see Backstamp 8. This would indicate that ware showing the 'A' as part of the backstamp was made after the war years.

Explanation of Backstamps

Backstamp 1: WINTON WARE GRIMWADES STOKE ON TRENT ENGLAND. Grimwades backstamp c1906+. Also found without the words WINTON WARE. The mark shows the globe which is sometimes found surmounted by a crown and accompanied by the letters GB for Grimwade Brothers c1885+.

Backstamp 2: GRIMWADES ROYAL WINTON WARE c1917-19+.

Backstamp 3: GRIMWADES S.P. STAFFS MADE IN ENGLAND c1922+. The letters S.P. stand for Semi-Porcelain.

Backstamp 4: ROYAL WINTON GRIMWADES ENGLAND. Art Deco style mark c1928+ found on items including Marguerite chintz. This mark was previously thought to date from the mid-1930s.

Backstamp 5: ROYAL WINTON GRIMWADES MADE IN ENGLAND. Art deco style mark c1934+. Note the semi-circular MADE IN ENGLAND mark also present. This can sometimes be found alone, transfer printed in either green and black, and with no other Royal Winton backstamp.

Backstamp 6: ROYAL WINTON GRIMWADES ENGLAND. Art Deco style mark c1937+. This backstamp seems to have been used only on Quilt and Tartans. Note the registration numbers for Canada which appear to be a date.

Backstamp 7: Summertime COPYRIGHT Wright Tyndale & van Roden Inc ENGLAND. Blue transfer printed copyright mark in script and capitals, found only on some Summertime pieces.

Backstamp 8: Royal Winton MADE IN ENGLAND A. The script mark c1951+. Note the 'A' mark used from 1945. The illustration also shows the registration numbers for Canada, Australia, New Zealand and the USA transfer printed in gold.

Backstamp 9: Royal Winton GRIMWADES ENGLAND. The fine script mark transfer printed in black c1964+. This was the backstamp used by Royal Winton after the takeover by Howards.

Backstamp 10: J-W Co. STAFFORDSHIRE ENGLAND ROYAL WINTON. This is a mystery backstamp, possibly used by the Staffordshire Potteries after they took over Royal Winton in 1979.

Backstamp 11: ATLAS CHINA STOKE ON TRENT GRIMWADES ENGLAND. Grimwades backstamp found on a Marguerite cup and saucer. The word Grimwades spans the globe carried by Atlas. This mark was used from 1910 onwards until it was replaced by a stylised mark similar to Backstamp 4 c1934-39

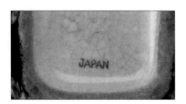

Backstamp 12: JAPAN. The word is transfer printed in red with no other identifying backstamp. This implies that Japanese copies were made and imported into the UK, and that the pattern is not by Royal Winton.

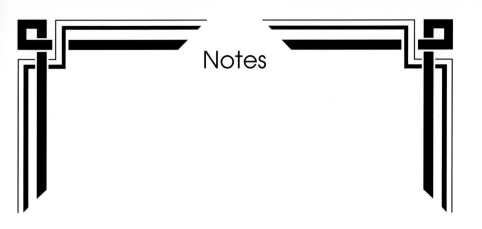

Notes

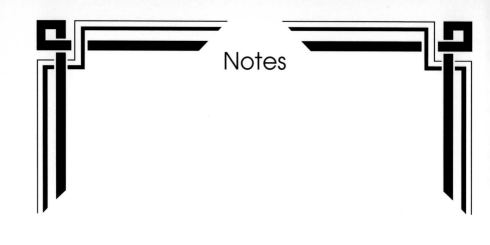

Notes

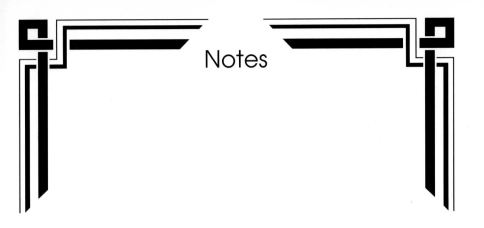

Notes

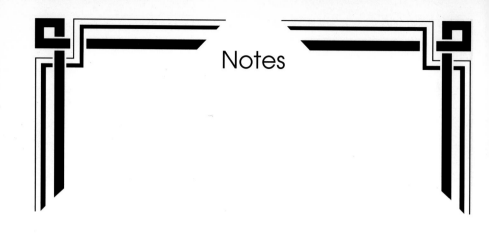

Notes

Francis Joseph
Collector's Register

Join the **Francis Joseph Royal Winton Chintz Collectors Register**. Registration is free and you will receive a newsletter twice yearly with news of auctions, events, sales and new publications on your particular collecting interest.

Join our register listing your top ten Royal Winton Chintz designs by filling in the form provided or write to:

The Francis Joseph Royal Winton Chintz Collectors Register,
15 St Swithuns Road, London SE13 6RW
or to
PO Box Box 69, 4763 Miami FL33269, USA